Working with Students Who Have Anxiety

As the number of students with anxiety increases in schools and classrooms, this book serves as the go-to guide for teachers and educators who strive to provide a welcoming environment conducive to students' learning. *Working with Students Who Have Anxiety* provides an accessible understanding of anxiety in its various forms, how anxiety impacts academic and social skills, and what teachers can do to create a positive climate. An exciting new resource for teachers, special educators, art specialists, and school counselors, this book covers the causes, signs, and symptoms of anxiety; includes academic, behavioral, and art-based interventions; and explores ethical and legal issues relating to students with anxiety. Filled with real-life examples, practical teaching tips, and creative advice for building connections with students, this book not only provides readers with the latest information about anxiety but also focuses on strategies to give educators the real tools they need to reduce the negative impact of anxiety in academic settings.

Beverley H. Johns is a Learning and Behavior Consultant, and Professional Fellow at MacMurray College, Jacksonville, IL, USA.

Donalyn Heise is an Art Education Consultant specializing in art for fostering resilience in students who have experienced trauma and Founder and Co-Director of Teacher Effectiveness for Art Learning (TEAL).

Adrienne D. Hunter is a pioneer in teaching art to in-crisis, at-risk, and incarcerated students, and is Past President of the Special Needs in Art Education (SNAE) interest group within the National Art Education Association (NAEA).

Other Eye on Education Books

Available from Routledge
(www.routledge.com/eyeoneducation)

For more information about this series, please visit: https://www.routledge.com

Working with Students Who Have Anxiety

Creative Connections and Practical Strategies

Beverley H. Johns

Donalyn Heise

Adrienne D. Hunter

Routledge
Taylor & Francis Group

NEW YORK AND LONDON

First published 2020
by Routledge
52 Vanderbilt Avenue, New York, NY 10017

and by Routledge
2 Park Square, Milton Park, Abingdon, Oxon, OX14 4RN

Routledge is an imprint of the Taylor & Francis Group, an informa business

Library of Congress Cataloging-in-Publication Data
A catalog record for this title has been requested

ISBN: 978-0-367-13867-7 (hbk)
ISBN: 978-0-367-13868-4 (pbk)
ISBN: 978-0-429-02897-7 (ebk)

Typeset in Palatino
by codeMantra
Visit the eResources: www.routledge.com/9780367138684

To all children who have experienced anxiety and to the families and educators who support them.

Contents

Meet the Authors

Beverley Holden Johns, MS Ed, Special Education, is a learning and behavior consultant, and Professional Fellow at MacMurray College, Jacksonville, Illinois. She has 40 years' experience working with students with learning disabilities (LD) and/or emotional/behavioral disorders (EBD) within the public schools. She was the founder and administrator of the Garrison Alternative School for students with severe EBD in Jacksonville, Illinois. Johns is the lead author of 15 books (and co-author of five others). She is co-author, with Janet Lerner, of the seminal college LD textbook *Learning Disabilities and Related Disabilities* (13th ed.). She is the 2000 recipient of the International Council for Exceptional Children (CEC) Outstanding Leadership Award, Past International President of the Council for Children with Behavioral Disorders, Past President of the CEC Pioneers, Past Secretary and Governmental Relations Chair for the Division for Learning Disabilities, and 2007 Recipient of the Romaine P. Mackie Leadership Service Award. She is listed in Who's Who in America, Who's Who of American Women, Who's Who in American Education, and Who's Who among America's Teachers. She has presented workshops across the United States and Canada; San Juan, Puerto Rico; Sydney, Australia (keynote); Warsaw, Poland; Wroclaw, Poland (keynote); Hong Kong, China; Lima, Peru; and Riga, Latvia. She is a graduate of Catherine Spalding College in Louisville, Kentucky, and received a fellowship for her graduate work at Southern Illinois University (SIU) in Carbondale, Illinois, where she received an MS in Special Education. She has done post-graduate work at the University of Illinois, Western Illinois University, SIU, and Eastern Illinois University.

Donalyn Heise, Ed D., is an Art Education Consultant who specializes in art for fostering resilience in students who have experienced trauma. She has been an artist and educator for more than 30 years in K-12 public and private schools, and several universities. As Associate Professor of Art Education at the

University of Memphis, she conducted research on the transformative power of art and community art collaborations. Dr. Heise designed and conducted over 100 professional development workshops and presentations at the state, national, and international levels. She served as Director for the Center for Innovation in Art Education; Director of Education for the Paul R. Williams Project; President of the Tennessee Art Education Association; President of the Nebraska Art Teachers Association; founding board member of the Nebraska Alliance for Art; and Founder and Co-Director of Teacher Effectiveness for Art Learning, an affiliate of Advanced Learning, Inc. As Art and Technology Coordinator for ConferNet, she designed, implemented, and evaluated professional development for six school districts and coordinated one of the nation's first virtual art-based academic K-16 conferences. Awards include the 2013 Tennessee Special Needs Art Educator of the Year Award; 2010 Tennessee Art Educator of the Year; 2010 NAEA Southeastern Region Higher Education Award; 2009 National Art Education Association, VSA-CEC Beverly Levett Gerber Special Needs Lifetime Achievement Award; 2007 Tennessee Higher Ed Art Educator of the Year; and 1997 Nebraska Art Teachers' Association Supervisor/Administrator of the Year Award. Selected publications include *Children in Crisis: Transforming Fear into Hope Through Multimodal Literacy, Community Art for Youth with Disabilities*, "Preparing competent art teachers for urban schools," "Steeling and resilience in art education," *Transforming Pain into Peace Through the Power of Art*, and *Fostering Resilience in An Intergenerational Art and Literacy Program in a Shelter for Families Who Are Homeless.*

Adrienne D. Hunter, M Ed, Special Education, is a pioneer in teaching art to in-crisis, at-risk, and incarcerated students. Recently retired, she was an art teacher in the Allegheny Intermediate Unit Alternative Education Program in Pittsburgh, Pennsylvania, for over 35 years. Hunter designed and implemented fully inclusive art curriculums for students, ages 6–21, from homeless shelters, crisis centers, alternative education high schools, and maximum security institutions. Through her sensitive and innovative curricula, she has addressed issues of gangs, domestic violence, homelessness, substance abuse, mental illness, and death while creating a safe haven for inner city youth through art. Hunter's commitment to education and advocacy extends far beyond the workplace. She has reached across racial, generational, economic, and community boundaries to form partnerships with colleges and universities, senior citizen centers, day care centers, local merchants, news media, and community agencies throughout Allegheny County to guide her students in creating positive contributions in their communities and healing through art. She is a nationally recognized presenter and an internationally exhibited fiber artist. She is the recipient of numerous awards and grants, including a Fulbright Memorial Fund Teacher Scholarship to study art and education in Japan; the National Art Education Association (NAEA), Very Special Arts (VSA), Council for Exceptional Children (CEC), Beverly Levett Gerber Special Needs Art Educator Lifetime Achievement Award (2016); the inaugural NAEA/Special Needs Art Educator of the Year Award (2008); and the Pennsylvania Art Education Association (PAEA) Outstanding Secondary Art Educator of the Year Award (1996). Hunter is a Past-President of the NAEA/ Special Needs Art Educators. She holds a Bachelor of Fine Arts from Pratt Institute, Brooklyn, New York, and a Master of Education from Duquesne University, Pittsburgh, Pennsylvania. She is Pennsylvania state certified to teach Art K-12, Elementary Education, and Special Education. She is lead editor with Donalyn Heise and Beverley H. Johns of *Art for Children Experiencing Psychological Trauma*, a Routledge publication. Hunter co-authored "Identifying the Visually Gifted: A Case Study" in *Art, Science, & Visual Literacy* and the "Teacher's Assessment Resource Booklet" for the "Students with Emotional and/or Behavior Disorders" in NAEA *Reaching and Teaching Students with Special Needs through Art*.

Preface

How can educators assist students who worry frequently, become fearful in academic settings, or become physically ill at the thought of taking a test? These challenges are faced every day by educators as they strive to meet the needs of their students. Not all of these students have diagnosed anxiety disorders, but they face fears, worries, and stressors that are interfering with learning.

Anxiety is the most prevalent mental health disorders among children and adolescents (Killu & Crundwell, 2016). Twenty-five percent of children between the ages of 13 and 18 have an anxiety disorder (McKibben, 2017). Anxiety can negatively affect a child's academic success. Addressing the social and emotional needs of children can reverse negative impacts of anxiety.

Teachers are often the first to notice signs and symptoms of anxiety in students. Protecting them may include determining whether the symptoms reflect trauma or abuse. Many educators report a lack of knowledge and resources required to assess and successfully meet the needs of students who are anxious. Having a basic understanding of anxiety, with effective strategies to address issues, may help students become more resilient.

Positive relationships, effective academic and behavioral intervention, and innovative creative arts can reduce the negative impact of anxiety on students.

The authors of this book have a combined expertise in the field of art, education, and special education. They continue to serve as teachers, researchers, and leaders in the field. The content of this book is based on their vast experiences and research data. The authors conducted interviews with students who have experienced anxiety as well as parents and teachers. Quotes from these interviews are included in the book; names have been changed to protect the identity of the contributors.

This book provides educators and school professionals a basic understanding of anxiety in its various forms. Throughout the book, academic, behavioral, and art-based interventions built on best practices are provided. These can be used by special educators, art specialists, general educators, school counselors, and other school-based professionals.

Part I defines anxiety and describes types of anxiety, specifically those commonly experienced by students. Causes, signs, and symptoms are included in this section.

Part II focuses on assessing students to plan positive behavioral interventions, including preventive techniques.

Part III focuses on ethical and legal issues that impact children with anxiety disorders, including privacy and student rights. Information is provided to guide educators as they assess impact of anxiety on education performance that warrants special education services or specific accommodations through a Section 504 plan under the Rehabilitation Act of 1973.

Finally, Part IV provides a bibliography of resources, including books, web resources, and organizations.

This book not only provides readers with the latest information about anxiety but also focuses on strategies that are designed to give educators the tools they need to meet the needs of students who are facing real-life anxiety.

REFERENCES

Killu, K., & Crundwell, R. (2016). Students with anxiety in the classroom: Educational accommodations and Interventions. *Beyond Behavior, 25(2)*, 28–39.

McKibben, S. (2017). Helping ease student anxiety. *ASCD Education Update, 59(8)*, 1, 4–5.

Rehabilitation Act. (1973). Section 504, 29 U. S. C. section 701, et seq.

Acknowledgments

With special gratitude to Cathy Gerhold for her invaluable assistance in preparing and editing this manuscript.

With thanks to DeeAnn Roome, MacMurray College Librarian, for all of her support and assistance in locating some of the references in this book.

With thanks to Beverly Levett Gerber, a lifelong advocate for children with special needs, for bringing us together and inspiring us to write this book.

And to Heather Jarrow, our Routledge editor, who had faith and confidence in our idea for this book. We are so appreciative of your support and assistance.

PART I
The Scope of Anxiety in Today's Schools

1

Understanding Anxiety

I'm nervous, but I don't understand why.

Female Student

LIVE FROM THE CLASSROOM

Mrs. Holden has been teaching fifth grade for over 16 years. It is now November, and, in her class of 26 students, she is concerned that three of them seem to over-react to what she perceives as small things. Laura is afraid of getting her clothes dirty and worries that she won't get an "A" on every test. Then there is Jaden, whose family lost all their belongings in a flood two months ago. When it rains, he starts shaking and asks to go to the nurse's office. Mrs. Holden is not sure whether she should allow him to go every time. She has another girl in her class, Betina, who starts crying when an adult male comes into the room. This is particularly concerning to Mrs. Holden as she wonders about possible abuse causing this anxiety. To her knowledge, none of these children have been diagnosed with an anxiety disorder, but she wonders whether they have one. She is worried and stressed about what she should be doing for these children.

Mrs. Holden is expressing a concern that is becoming more common in today's schools. Children may be stressed about their clothes getting dirty, being late for school, or family members being deported. Teachers feel ill-equipped to effectively deal with the rise in students who exhibit worry, fear, and anxiety.

Introduction

An increasing number of children have worries and fears, some to the point that it prohibits them from learning. Egger and Angold (2006) argue that anxiety disorders are common in preschool children. Younger children's worries focus on their being hungry or whether other children will play with them. Some young children cannot verbally express why they are stressed, but their actions reveal their worry, fear, and panic. Older students worry about friendships, being late, doing well in their classes, testing, and feeling pressured to get good scores and get into the colleges/universities they or their parents want. Sehgal, Jeffries, and Rappaport (2017–2018) identify racism and discrimination as a reason some students have anxiety.

Identified anxiety disorders are on the rise and are the most common mental health problems exhibited in children (Pella, Drake, Tein, & Ginsburg, 2017). The most common anxiety disorder is a specific phobia, the next most common is separation anxiety, and the next is social phobia (Hansen, Oerbeck, Skirbekk, & Kristensen, 2016), all of which will be described in this book.

The chapter also discusses the relationship between anxiety and emotional regulation. It discusses the reality of anxiety disorders and what those mean for educators in our schools.

Problems with Identification

There are problems with identification of children with anxiety. The complexity of comorbidity, the presence of two or more disorders occurring at the same time, may be a factor. For example, obsessive-compulsive disorder (OCD) and anxiety commonly occur together (Rozenman et al., 2017). Because the child exhibits oppositional defiant disorder (ODD) or another externalizing behavior, the concern is about ODD and not about anxiety. Parents and educators may miss anxiety symptoms. The child may not always be overtly exhibiting them. In a sample of 407 children referred for mental health problems, only 25 percent had anxiety as a referral symptom (Hansen, Oerbeck, Skirbekk, & Kristensen, 2016).

Kauffman and Brigham (2009) provide guidance as to when a teacher should or should not be concerned. Children who have disorders exhibit problematic behaviors far more often in a given period of time than typically developing children; engage in these behaviors in more varied settings, not just at school or on the bus; and exhibit these behaviors over a longer period of time. Their pattern of behavior is also ongoing, not transient.

Kauffman and Badar (2018) recognize that most people know that the longer you allow a physical problem to go before treating it, the more difficult it is to treat, yet people do not understand that the same is true for mental health issues. There is still a major stigma and shame attached to mental health disorders.

What Does This Mean in the Classroom?

How does a teacher decide to intervene? When teachers notice concerning patterns of behavior, documenting these behaviors may help to determine their frequency, whether they are continuous, and whether they occur over a long period of time. These logs may also exhibit whether more than one behavior is occurring, e.g., worry, fear, stress, and anxiety. The logs may help in deciding whether or not to act by discussing the student with other teachers, the principal, social workers, school psychologists, nurses, guidance counselors, or parents.

If it is decided to speak with parents, a teacher is not being judgmental about what is going on in the home but instead is reporting to the parents the concerning behaviors that are occurring at school and determining whether these behaviors are isolated or also happening at home.

Definitions

Worry Defined

Everyone worries at some time. It may be about paying bills, being late for an event, or whether a past decision was thought to be appropriate by others. Worrisome thoughts are a normal part of life, but when worry interferes with life functioning, it becomes a sign for intervention. The child who is worried he might make a mistake on an assignment may refuse to do the assignment. The child who is worried no one will want to sit next to him in the cafeteria at lunch finds excuses for not wanting to eat lunch. The most common content of worrying is related to school, health, and social contacts (Muris, Meesters, Merckelbach, Sermon, & Zwakhalen, 1998).

Worry can be defined as "the dynamic cognitive component of anxiety" (Caes, Fisher, Clinch, Tobias, & Eccleston, 2016, p. 390). Worry is a normal part of childhood, and it changes as the child develops. The complexity and elaboration of worrisome thoughts increase from age eight. In a longitudinal study about children with worrisome thoughts, it was found that parents reported a peak of worrisome thoughts at the age of 10. The highest level of interference with a child's daily life was at age 13. As a result, distinguishing between pathological and normal forms of worrying is difficult.

The main feature of Generalized Anxiety Disorder (GAD) is "excessive and uncontrollable worry" (Esbjorn et al., 2015, p. 145). The child's state of mind is focused on negative self-thoughts (Wells & Carter, 1999).

What Does This Mean in the Classroom?

Teachers can look for signs that a student is engaging in worrying behaviors, impacting their ability to socialize or perform academic tasks. Providing and modeling positive self-talk and having students practice it is a good strategy.

Fear, Rational and Irrational, Defined

At times, a sense of fear is rational. Children may be afraid of jumping off a diving board because they are afraid they are not good swimmers and might drown. They are afraid of talking to strangers because their parents and teachers have told them that this may be dangerous. Childhood fears are common (Dalrymple-Alford & Salmon, 2015; Kushnir & Sadeh, 2010). Other fears are irrational. A child is afraid of participating in a recreational dance class because she does not know what to do; however, explaining to her that in the class, the teacher will teach her how to do dance movements does not calm her panic attack. When fears interfere with daily life and inhibit children's development, it can be a problem that needs to be addressed.

Children who have higher levels of internalizing problems display a range of social, emotional, and behavioral characteristics that include fearfulness, anxiety, and behavioral inhibition (Zahn-Waxler, Klimes-Dougan, & Slattery, 1999). Children who have higher levels of externalizing behavior tend to seek excitement or to stimulate sensations (Rothbart & Ahadi, 1994).

Attention to threat in fear-inducing situations has been linked with outcomes such as shyness or social inhibition. Young children who are prone to fear use hypervigilance as a means of regulating their behavior, but this has been found to be ineffective in reducing distress as children age (Hummel, Premo, & Kiel, 2017).

Normally, children progress developmentally from concrete fears in childhood, like animals, loud noises, or darkness, to abstract fears in adolescence, such as social criticism or schoolwork, to global fears, such as money or political concerns in late adolescence. Fears typically decrease as children get older (Richman, Dotson, Rose, Thompson, & Abby, 2012).

The terms "fear" and "anxiety" have been used synonymously but are quite different. The most common fears of 8–13-year-old students are related to physical harm or animals. In one study, it was found that children with higher fear levels were not as successful when working on memory tasks and had slower motor responses than students who did not have such fear. Children with higher fear levels also reported more somatic complaints, i.e., having to do with the body as opposed to the mind. Older children reported more fears than younger children, and girls demonstrated higher levels of fears than boys (Caes, Fisher, Clinch, Tobias, & Eccleston, 2016; Kushnir & Sadeh, 2010).

It is thought that confirmation bias is relevant to the onset of anxiety disorders (Dibbets, Fliek, & Meesters, 2015). Confirmation bias means that one who is fearful of something has a tendency to selectively search for information confirming that fear while ignoring information that disconfirms the threat. These children have a higher chance of developing anxiety, which, if left unchecked, can turn into anxiety disorders.

What Does This Mean in the Classroom?

When a student repeatedly says they do not feel well and asks to go to the school nurse or bathroom, an educator can investigate whether the child has a physical problem or is dealing with fears of which the teacher may not be aware. Talk to students about their fears and how to face them. Use of visual and performing arts, such as storytelling, movement exercises, or puppetry, may be helpful. Teachers should be concerned when fears seem to linger beyond a normal age, such as older students who are still afraid of loud noises or darkness.

Stress Defined

Daily stressors in children are grouped into three major fear areas: school, health, and family (Rodriquez, Torres, Paez, & Ingles, 2016). Children may worry about performing a task in front of other students or are stressed by the behavior of other students. Children may become stressed at the thought of going to the doctor or perceive they have something wrong with them. Finally, students may be stressed about their home situation: parental illness, yelling or fighting, or fear they might be separated from family members.

It was found that students with specific learning disabilities had lower levels of resilience than those with borderline intellectual function, meaning they had inadequate inner coping skills. Students with borderline intellectual functioning had higher levels of resilience (Panicker & Chelliah, 2016).

Shang, Li, Li, Wang, and Siegrist (2014) discussed the effects of school-related stress on students both in North America and in China, and found that there was a higher prevalence of suicidal thoughts and stronger effects from a stressful psychosocial school environment on high school students than on middle school students.

The presence of chronic psychosocial stress is a public health threat; it has been associated with a higher energy intake related to emotionally based eating of comfort food rich in sugar and fat, possibly causing the child to become obese (Michels, Sioen, Ruige, & Henauw, 2017). Stress occurs when the demands of situations exceed an individual's ability to cope and resolve the problematic situation.

What Does This Mean in the Classroom?

When children are experiencing stress, teachers need to be calm, supportive, and respectful. When planning activities, give consideration to whether they may result in stress and, if so, rethink the activity. Allowing students to tell or write a story about their feelings may reduce their stress. Reading or listening to stories about other children who have experienced stress and have overcome it may also be helpful (Cole, 2015). Stories using imaginary characters or animals that model resilience may provide a comfortable, non-threatening environment for the child to discuss successful coping strategies.

Stress can be avoided when teams are chosen by having the students count off rather than being selected by a team captain. Educators can also be alert to the eating habits of students to determine whether they are engaging in stress-related eating. Any concerns should be noted and discussed with parents or support personnel.

Anxiety Defined

Anxiety in certain given situations is a normal emotion experienced by most people. Children may exhibit anxiety when they do not feel in control. Children go through stages where they may be more anxious than usual. Some children, when faced with a difficult event, may engage in catastrophizing thoughts, but after a period of time, they no longer have those thoughts. All children learn to live with some anxiety, but some need the assistance of supportive educators and parents to provide comforting and supportive environments, and to move forward. Anxiety that interferes with the child's ability to engage in activities and occurs over a specific period of time is of concern (Fritz, 2011).

There are children who exhibit a specific anxiety about a certain subject, such as math. Rubinstein and Tannock (2010) define mathematics anxiety as "a negative reaction to math associated with negative emotions" (p. 1). Anxiety threatens self-concept, causing tension, helplessness, and even dread.

Reading anxiety has been found to be a prominent characteristic of inadequate responders to reading interventions (Grills et al., 2014). Children with learning disabilities often have reading problems and are at risk of experiencing anxiety and depression (Gallegos, Langley, & Villegas, 2012).

Test anxiety is exhibited by many students as this society has become more test-driven (Johns, 2016). In 2003, Casbarro coined the term "post traumatic test disorder" (Johns, 2016, p. vii). Stress over taking tests can result in fear of failure, avoidance, difficulty concentrating, and an increase in anxiety about school. More on test anxiety will be covered in the next chapter.

What Does This Mean in the Classroom?

It is helpful to keep a log of anxiety behaviors to track their frequency and duration. Providing children an opportunity to write or draw about their anxiety, without the fear of criticism, is a healthy alternative to stress. Relaxation exercises and mindful breathing techniques are designed to reduce anxiety. Quiet the room, or play soft instrumental music, and ask students to close their eyes, relax their bodies, focus on their breathing, and allow moments of silence. Mindfulness activities can promote self-management for students. Such strategies enable a student to be less reactive to emotional stimuli (Minkos, Chafouleas, Bray, & LaSalle, 2018).

When educators observe students catastrophizing, work to refocus the child's attention on the positive by having them write a list of all the possible positive outcomes.

Anxiety Disorder Defined

How does an anxiety disorder differ from worry, fear, stress, or signs of anxiety? A disorder is defined by its excessiveness or persistence beyond developmentally appropriate periods. Disorders differ from a transient fear or anxiety that may be stress-induced by lasting six months or more, although the *Diagnostic and statistical manual, Fifth Edition* (DSM-5) tells us this is only a general guide (American Psychiatric Association, 2013). Anxiety disorders develop during childhood and persist if not treated. Anxiety disorders are a major mental health concern because they can be associated with deviant conduct, substance abuse, and depression, and can interfere with school, social, and family functioning (Gallegos, Langley, & Villegas, 2012).

Anxiety disorders are diagnosed only when the presenting symptoms cannot be attributed to the physiological effects of either a substance or a medication, or cannot be better explained by another mental disorder (American Psychiatric Association, 2013). Research has found that a difficult temperament at the age of five months was a strong predictor of depression and anxiety symptoms, while maternal depression was the second-most important predictor of a child's depression and anxiety symptoms (Cote et al., 2009).

What Does This Mean in the Classroom?

Children should feel safe in a classroom. Teachers can identify, in advance, support personnel available to assist children. Teachers can review social developmental studies done with the child to determine if there is a history of difficult temperament and maternal depression.

Emotional Regulation and Managing Stress Defined

The ability to maintain and control one's emotions is a significant factor in managing one's stress and anxiety. Children and adolescents who experienced stress in their early lives in institutional care, who were not provided sufficient care, attention, or support from parents or other caregivers, had emotional regulation deficits later in childhood or adolescence (Burkholder, Koss, Hostinar, Johnson, & Gunnar, 2016).

Early-life stress plays an important role and requires early intervention to promote a child or an adolescent's ability to regulate their expression of anxiety. It may produce lasting problems if not addressed (Burkholder, Koss, Hostinar, Johnson, & Gunnar, 2016).

The ability to modulate and manage emotional experiences in ways that promote healthy functioning is critical in preventing some types of anxiety. Youth with OCD showed lower levels of emotional regulation than those with other anxiety disorders. These youth utilize ineffective coping strategies when they have distressing emotions (Jacob, Morelen, Suveg, Jacobsen, & Whiteside, 2012).

Coping strategies are conscious and voluntary efforts used to regulate emotions and behaviors in response to the stress of everyday events. Some children cope in an unhealthy way by concealing the problem; strategies of active solution are related to high adaptation and psychological well-being. The ability to problem solve is related to high adaptation (Rodriguez, Torres, Paez, & Ingles, 2016).

What Does This Mean in the Classroom?

It is important that teachers model and teach effective coping strategies and methods of regulating emotions. Perhaps talking to someone, deep breathing, or taking their own time-out to calm down will be useful. In addition, teachers can teach critical and creative thinking to strengthen effective problem-solving, which helps to promote successful adaptation.

TEN TEACHING TIPS

1. If a child is exhibiting anxiety, keep logs of patterns of behavior.
2. Talk with support personnel at school and to parents to determine whether they are seeing the same problematic behaviors.
3. Teach students deep breathing and mindfulness activities.
4. Provide supportive comments to students when first seen engaging in worrying behaviors.
5. If a student is seen to be overeating or exhibiting somatic complaints, try to pinpoint any stress.
6. Refocus the student on positive events when you see them engaging in excessive worry.
7. When students are becoming anxious, provide an outlet for them to express their worries or fears, such as writing a story or drawing a picture.
8. Read stories to children about how characters have overcome stress.
9. Model effective coping strategies.
10. Ensure that the classroom is a safe and worry-free environment for all students.

Creative Connections

Emotions

The ability to manage emotions is a significant factor in managing one's stress. Educators are not clinical therapists. Throughout this book, we provide strategies that are within an educator's scope of practice.

For young children who don't understand emotions, *The Way I Feel* by Janan Cain is a good book with great pictures about emotions. After reading it to the children, they can try making faces that display emotions. Having mirrors available for the children to see themselves as they make emotional faces is not only fun but also helpful in teaching them to read faces. For older children, it can be made into a game, where they chose a piece of paper from a bag on which an emotion is written and then act out the emotion, like playing charades.

Monsters Who Eat Fear

Pre-K to Six

Very young children enjoy playing peek-a-boo, which is a fun activity that can lead up to BOO! and then to being scared. There are great children's books with beautiful illustrations that focus on fear and can serve as a lead-in for the following art project. *What Do You Do with A Problem?* written by Kobi Yamada and illustrated by Mae Besom is a story about worry and what happens when you have a problem, facing it, and finding an opportunity for something good. Another recommended book is *Courage*, written and illustrated by Bernard Weber, which addresses courage, what it is, and different kinds of courage, and gives examples of courage. Take caution in selecting books, nothing too scary, gory, or bloody, and keep in mind that for some children who have been abused, something in the story might trigger a meltdown.

After reading a story pertaining to fear, and giving the children a chance to make comments or display fearful faces or actions, have the children draw a monster whose job it will be to "Eat the Student's Fear"! Another variation on this theme is to have the children make monster pinch pots out of clay. The clay monster pots can then be used to dispose of one's fears. There are some air-drying clay products on the market as well as easy-to-make homemade playdough recipes online made with inexpensive, simple ingredients.

Middle and High School

By this age, students have probably seen many scary movies, and a guided discussion can be started about the movies they may have seen. Again, the conversation should be redirected from becoming too macabre. For this activity, students will create their own monsters.

Materials

From a large roll of craft paper, cut student-sized sheets, or if that is not possible, use the largest size paper available. Other materials needed are pencils; paint; markers; glue; magazines; and a plethora of supplies, such as glitter, feathers, scraps of fabric, yarn, and found objects. Using large sheets of craft paper, have the students trace a rough outline around their bodies with pencil. They can work in pairs to accomplish this task. Have a few pre-traced figures for those who may not wish to be traced. Tracing can occur by having the student lie on the paper, hanging the paper on the wall and having the student stand in front of it, or shining a bright light to cast a shadow to trace. Some students may even wish to just draw their own shapes. Once the shapes are drawn, have the students make the shapes into monsters, who will then eat all of their worries and fears! They can use paint, markers, or collage, or even embellish the shapes with a variety of small objects. Encourage the students to be as creative as possible to be sure that their monster is up for the task of gobbling up all that fear! Students at this age may have a tendency to get very graphic with blood and gore, so before starting the art exercise, be specific about what will be permitted and what will not.

If space is an issue, the students can draw monsters on more manageably sized paper and still get creative with their monsters. Since these are public monsters, it is not recommended that the students be asked to write their particular fears on the monsters. However, if the students, on their own and without encouragement, write generic fears on their monsters as part of their artistic expression and design, this may be permitted.

Create a display of the monsters in the classroom or hallway to validate students' worries, fears, and anxieties.

KEY TAKEAWAYS

- ♦ Classroom teachers are first responders when students are in need of help for anxiety.

- ♦ Children with cognitive bias have a greater chance of developing anxiety disorders.

- ♦ Fear can result in an increase in somatic complaints, poor working memory, and motor problems.

- ♦ Stress can result in overeating, leading to obesity and other health-related issues.

- ♦ Difficult temperament as early as five months of age and maternal depression are strong indicators of depression and anxiety symptoms.

REFERENCES

American Psychiatric Association. (2013). *Diagnostic and Statistical Manual of Mental Disorders* (5th ed.). Washington, DC: American Psychiatric Publishing.

Burkholder, A., Koss, K., Hostinar, C., Johnson, A., & Gunnar, M. (2016). Early life stress: Effects on the regulation of anxiety expression in children and adolescents. *Social Development, 25(4),* 777–793.

Caes, L., Fisher, E., Clinch, J., Tobias, J., & Eccleston, C. (2016). The development of worry throughout childhood: Avon longitudinal study of parents and children data. *British Journal of Health Psychology, 21,* 389–406.

Cain, J. (2000). *The way I feel.* Seattle, WA: Parenting Press.

Casbarro, J. (2003). *Test anxiety and what you can do about it.* Port Chester, NY: Dude, a Division of National Professional Resources.

Cole, E. (2015). Understanding post-traumatic stress in children and adolescents. *Baltic Journal of Psychology, 16(1)*, 90–97.

Cote, S., Boivin, M., Liu, X., Nagin, D., Zoccolillo, M., & Tremblay, R. (2009). Depression and anxiety symptoms: Onset, developmental course and risk factors during early childhood. *The Journal of Child Psychology and Psychiatry, 50(10)*, 1201–1208.

Dalrymple-Alford, S., & Salmon, K. (2015). Ambiguous information and the verbal information pathway to fear in children. *Journal of Child and Family Studies, 24*, 679–686.

Dibbets, P., Fliek, L., & Meesters, C. (2015). Fear-related confirmation bias in children: A comparison between neutral- and dangerous-looking animals. *Child Psychiatry and Human Development, 46*, 418–425.

Egger, H., & Angold, A. (2006). Common emotional and behavioral disorders in preschool children: Presentation, nosology, and epidemiology. *Journal of Child Psychology and Psychiatry, 47(3/4)*, 313–337.

Esbjorn, B., Lonfeldt, N., Nielsen, S., Reinholdt-Dunne, M., Somhovd, M., & Cartwright-Hatton, S. (2015). Meta-worry, worry, and anxiety in children and adolescents: Relationships and Interactions. *Journal of Clinical Child and Adolescent Psychology, 4(1)*, 145–156.

Fritz, G. (Ed.). (2011). Does your child have an anxiety disorder? *The Brown University Child and Adolescent Behavior Letter, 27(S3)*, I–II.

Gallegos, J., Langley, A., & Villegas, D. (2012). Anxiety, depression, and coping skills among Mexican school children: A comparison of students with and without learning disabilities. *Learning Disability Quarterly, 35(1)*, 54–61.

Grills, A., Fletcher, J., Vaughn, S., Barth, A., Denton, C., & Stuebing, K. (2014). Anxiety and response to reading intervention among first grade students. *Child Youth Care Forum, 43*, 417–431.

Hansen, B., Oerbeck, B., Skirbekk, B., & Kristensen, H. (2016). Non-obsessive-compulsive anxiety disorders in child and adolescent mental health services—Are they underdiagnosed, and how accurate is referral information? *Nord Journal of Psychiatry, 70(2)*, 133–139.

Hummel, A., Premo, J., & Kiel, E. (2017). Attention to threat as a predictor of shyness in the context of internalizing and externalizing behavior. *Infancy, 22(2)*, 240–255.

Jacob, M., Morelen, D., Suveg, C., Jacobsen, A., & Whiteside, S. (2012). Emotional, behavioral, and cognitive factors that differentiate obsessive-compulsive disorder and other anxiety disorders in youth. *Anxiety, Stress, and Coping, 25(2)*, 229–237.

Johns, B. (2016). *Preparing test-resistant students for assessment.* Palm Beach Gardens, FL: LRP Publications.

Kauffman, J., & Brigham, F. (2009). *Working with troubled children.* Verona, WI: Full Court Press.

Kauffman, J., & Badar, J. (2018). *The scandalous neglect of children's mental health: What schools can do.* New York, NY: Routledge.

Kushnir, J., & Sadeh, A. (2010). Childhood fears, neurobehavioral functioning and behavior problems in school-age children. *Child Psychiatry and Human Development, 41*, 88–97.

Michels, N., Sioen, I., Ruige, J., & Henauw, S. (2017). Children's psychosocial stress and emotional eating: A role for leptin? *International Journal of Eating Disorders, 50(5)*, 471–480.

Minkos, M., Chafouleas, S., Bray, M., & LaSalle, T. (2018). Brief report: A preliminary investigation of a mindful breathing intervention to increase academic engagement in an alternative educational setting. *Behavioral Disorders, 43(4)*, 436–443.

Muris, P., Meesters, C., Merckelbach, H., Sermon, A., & Zwakhalen, S. (1998). Worry in normal children. *Journal of the American Academy of Child and Adolescent Psychiatry, 37*, 703–710.

Panicker, A., & Chelliah, A. (2016). Resilience and stress in children and adolescents with specific learning disability. *Journal of the Canadian Academy of Child and Adolescent Psychiatry, 25(1)*, 17–23.

Pella, J., Drake, K., Tein, J., & Ginsburg, G. (2017). Child anxiety prevention study: Impact on functional outcomes. *Child Psychiatry and Human Development, 48*, 400–410.

Richman, D., Dotson, W., Rose, C., Thompson, S., & Abby, L. (2012). Effects of age on the types and severity of excessive fear or the absence of fear in children and young adults with autism. *Journal of Mental Health Research in Intellectual Disabilities, 5*, 215–235.

Rodriguez, F., Torres, M., Paez, J., & Ingles, C. (2016). Prevalence of strategies for coping with daily stress in children. *Psicothema, 28(4)*, 370–376.

Rothbart, M. & Ahadi, S. (1994). Temperament and the development of personality. *Journal of Abnormal Psychology, 103*, 55.

Rozenman, M., Peris, T, Bergman, L., Chang, S., O'Neill, J., McCracken, J., & Piacentini, J. (2017). Distinguishing fear versus distress symptomology in pediatric OCD. *Child Psychiatry and Human Development, 48*, 63–72.

Rubinsten, O., & Tannock, R. (2010). Mathematics anxiety in children with developmental dyscalculia. *Behavioral and Brain Functions, 6(46)*, 1–13.

Sehgal, P., Jeffries, J., & Rappaport, N. (2017–2018). Combatting race-related stress in the classroom. *Educational Leadership, 75(4)*, 51–55.

Shang, L., Li, J., Li, Y., Wang, T., & Siegrist, J. (2014). Stressful psychosocial school environment and suicidal ideation in Chinese adolescents. *Social Psychiatry and Psychiatric Epidemiology, 49*, 205–210.

Wells, A., & Carter, K. (1999). Preliminary tests of a cognitive model of generalized anxiety disorder. *Behaviour Research and Therapy, 37*, 585–594.

Yamada, K. (2016). *What do you do with a problem?* Seattle, WA: Compendium Kids.

Zahn-Waxler, C., Klimes-Dougan, B., & Slattery M. (1999). Internalizing problems of childhood and adolescence: Prospects, pitfalls, and progress in understanding the development of anxiety and depression. *Development and Psychopathology, 12*, 443–466.

2

Types of Anxiety

My child always liked order. At a young age she wanted her toys returned to their proper places before she could go to sleep. She liked routines and functioned well within them. Teachers loved her because she followed the rules and never missed information. Substitute teachers have commented on how much easier it was because she knew all the class routines and where the teacher kept the supplies. She made good grades. However, ever since I was diagnosed with breast cancer, she has been obsessive!!! She freaks out if anything in her routine changes. Now in second grade she has trouble sleeping and is anxious every time there is a substitute. She wants me there for every field trip and cries often. It's so stressful.

A Parent

LIVE FROM THE CLASSROOM

Mr. Adorah teaches eighth-grade science. It is now March, and in November, his community saw significant damage from a hurricane. While no one died, many people lost their homes and were displaced. It was a very negative time for Mr. Adorah and his students who had to find new places to live, with some still living in temporary locations. Mr. Adorah found comfort in getting back to his normal routine when school reopened just a few days after the hurricane. He had talked with his students about their feelings and how he was upset about losing his condominium. Studying about hurricanes and their history helped him and many of his students. However, he has five students who are still very anxious. He talked with the other teachers and learned that these students are also anxious in their classes. When it begins to rain, they look like they are going to be sick and excuse themselves to go to the restroom. Their attendance has been sporadic. When Mr. Adorah talks to them privately about why they were not at school, they tell him that they are afraid to leave their parents in case there is another hurricane. They lack concentration in class and don't seem to care about whether they pass their classes. Mr. Adorah wonders what he should do. He has talked with the school social worker who shares his concerns. They question whether these students' reactions are normal or whether they need more intensive intervention. What is a natural time to grieve over a traumatic event? Why have most of the students seemed to bounce back, and these five have not?

This chapter discusses the many faces of anxiety as well as post-traumatic stress disorder (PTSD) and obsessive-compulsive disorder (OCD).

Trauma and Stressor-Related Disorders

In the *Diagnostic and Statistical Manual of Mental Disorders, Fifth Edition* (DSM-5) (American Psychiatric Association, 2013), trauma and other stressor-related disorders are separated from anxiety disorders. Teachers may find it difficult to differentiate these from anxiety disorders because of how the symptoms may present themselves. In keeping with the DSM-5, this chapter discusses Trauma and Stressor-Related Disorders separately in order to help educators differentiate between them and anxiety disorders, and to assist in determining what may be happening with a child. These are not easy distinctions to make.

Post-Traumatic Stress Disorder

Since the Vietnam War, much more has become known about PTSD. Many veterans who serve in war have difficulty talking about it. Some commit suicide. Some have lived with high levels of anxiety that have impacted their work and home life for years.

Schools are seeing an increase in children who have experienced some type of trauma and many other children who have experienced multiple traumatic events which have shaped their behavior as they come into the classroom. Children may have been sexually abused, physically abused, witnessed a shooting, lost their home to flooding or fire, or other major events. Traumatic events are becoming more common in childhood and adolescence. About 15% of students who have been exposed to traumatic events in their lives meet the diagnostic criteria for PTSD (Gutermann et al., 2016).

The prevalence may vary across development, but it can occur at any age beginning after the first year of life. PTSD usually begins within the first three months after the trauma, but it can be months or years before criteria for this diagnosis is met (American Psychiatric Association, 2013).

For children under six, they must have directly experienced the event or witnessed in person the event as it occurred to others, especially with a primary caregiver. Witnessing these events does not include events that are witnessed in electronic media, TV, pictures, or movies (American Psychiatric Association, 2013).

For a child over six to be diagnosed with PTSD, they must have directly experienced a traumatic event, witnessed an event in person that occurred to someone else, learned that a traumatic event occurred to a family member or friend who had a close relationship with them, or experienced repeated or extreme exposure to aversive events. The child over six may have recurring distressing memories, dreams, dissociative reactions such as flashbacks, intense psychological distress at exposure to internal or external cues that resemble the traumatic events, and physiological reactions to those events that resemble the event. They persistently avoid distressing memories and external reminders. They exhibit negative alterations in mood and cognitions, and have alterations in arousal and reactivity associated with the events. The duration is more than one month (Gutermann et al., 2016).

Unlike other anxiety disorders, PTSD is triggered by an external traumatic event. Objective characteristics of the traumatic event as well as the child's subjective experience of the event affect a child's risk of later developing PTSD (Swan, Cummings, Caporino, & Kendall, 2014).

Students may not have PTSD, but if they have experienced trauma, educators should be concerned about the impact this trauma is having on their lives. Traumatic experiences during childhood, especially those involving interpersonal violence, may have a profound impact on a child's functioning. Difficulty regulating emotions, self-blame, guilt, and shame are also prominent indicators of PTSD (Fletcher, 2011).

What Does This Mean in the Classroom?

Just because an event is over, and a few months have passed, this does not mean that the child is not going to have or develop PTSD. Some students in Mr. Adorah's class may begin experiencing difficulties a few months or years later. Providing assurances, safety within class, and giving students appropriate outlets for expressing their fear, worry, and stress are important.

The focus should be on strength and resilience-based interventions (Steele & Kuban, 2014); integrating academics and the arts gives students outlets to appropriately express their feelings.

Many of these children are in a state of constant alert. Educators should refrain from changes in structure and routine without preparation for those changes; avoid coming up from behind these students; some students will feel safer sitting in the back of the room so that they can see the other students.

OCD and Related Disorders

As is the case for trauma and other stress-related disorders, OCD has its own separate category in the DSM-5, although the manual does state that there are close relationships between anxiety disorders and OCD and related disorders (American Psychiatric Association, 2013). There is a large range of disorders within this category, including OCD, dysmorphia, hoarding, and hair-pulling and skin-picking disorder.

OCD presents itself with obsessions and/or compulsions. Obsessions are persistent and recurring thoughts, urges, or images that are intrusive and unwanted. Compulsions are repetitive behaviors that a child may feel driven to perform in response to an obsession or according to rigid rules. Common characteristics of OCD include cleaning over and over again, symmetry obsessions—making sure everything is in order, taboo thoughts, and fear of harm.

A body dysmorphic disorder is a preoccupation with perceived flaws in appearance and by repetitive behaviors such as excessive grooming (American Psychiatric Association, 2013).

Hoarding disorder is much more familiar to the general population since the beginning of the television show. It is a persistent difficulty in getting rid of items. Some have a problem with excessive acquisition, meaning that they collect, buy, or steal things.

Hair-pulling disorder refers to the recurrent pulling of one's hair, often resulting in hair loss, and repeated efforts to decrease or stop it.

With skin-picking disorder, there is the recurrent picking often resulting in skin lesions and repeated efforts to decrease the activity. Obsessions and/or compulsions can take up more than an hour a day.

According to the DSM-5 (American Psychiatric Association, 2013), the mean onset of OCD is 19½ years, although cases may start by age 14, and males may have onset before the age of 10. Onset in childhood or adolescence may result in a lifetime of affliction.

What Does This Mean in the Classroom?

Remember the child cannot control this behavior; anger by a teacher is not helpful. A child may want her papers to be in a specific order or work cannot be finished within a given time because it is not perfect. Accommodations may be needed. A student should never be embarrassed in front of his or her peers.

Cognitive and behavioral therapies have been found to be effective in the treatment of children with OCD. Students trapped in negative thinking can be taught to modify their dysfunctional thinking. This therapy is beyond what a teacher can provide, so it will be important to work closely with the child's therapists and parents. Behavioral therapy includes relaxation strategies, meditation, and biofeedback.

These children may be treated with medication. It will be important for educators to monitor any signs of side effects, improvement in the obsessive-compulsive behavior, or negative changes in behavior. The educator will want to report those changes to parents. Releases given by parents allow the educator to communicate observations directly with the child's doctor.

Anxiety Disorders

Anxiety disorders differ from normal fear, anxiety, or worry in that they are excessive, or they continue beyond developmentally appropriate periods of time. These disorders can manifest themselves in childhood and will persist if not treated. The educator plays a role in determining whether there are patterns of behavior that warrant a discussion with parents and a referral to other professionals. Females are more frequently referred for anxiety disorders (American Psychiatric Association, 2013).

An anxiety disorder is diagnosed by a qualified individual when the exhibited symptoms are not as a result of trauma, substance abuse, medication, other medical condition, or better explained by another mental disorder. Some of these anxiety disorders can overlap (American Psychiatric Association, 2013).

Panic Disorders

These are seen in children and adults when recurrent surges, intense fears, or discomforts reach a peak within minutes. During that time, four or more of the following symptoms are present: palpitations, trembling or shaking, shortness of breath, failure to breathe, fear that they are suffocating, feelings of choking, chest pain, nausea, stomachache, dizziness, chills or heat sensations, numbness or tingling, unreality or detachment, fear of losing control, freezing in place, or fear of dying. At least one attack is followed by one month or more of persistent worry about additional attacks and a major change in maladaptive behavior (American Psychiatric Association, 2013). The child may engage in avoidance behaviors to prevent a panic attack from recurring.

What Does This Mean in the Classroom?

Educators can watch for signs that the student is becoming fearful and make an attempt to remove the student from the situation that is causing the panic. If the student cannot be removed from the situation, the educator will need to stay calm and gently remind the student to engage in relaxation breathing. The student will need to hear reassuring statements that the educator is there with the student to help. To be respectful of the student, it is advisable to remove any audience.

Social Anxiety Disorder

Social anxiety disorder, also known as social phobia, is a serious fear or anxiety about social situations where the child is exposed to possible scrutiny by other people, e.g., giving a speech or meeting unfamiliar people. To be diagnosed with social anxiety disorder, it must occur in peer settings, not just adult interactions. In addition, the child fears that he will be negatively evaluated; the social situation provokes fear; and this fear might be expressed by crying, tantrums, freezing, clinging to someone, or failing to speak. The anxiety is out of proportion to the actual threat; it is persistent, lasting for six months or more; and causes distress in educational and social situations. The fear cannot be attributed to other physiological effects or another medical condition and is not better explained by another disorder, such as autism spectrum disorders.

It is considered performance based if the extreme fear is restricted to speaking or performing in public. Performance fears are manifested in school settings where public presentations are expected. Children with performance-only social anxiety disorders do not have the fear when they do not have to perform in front of others.

The degree and type of social anxiety disorder may vary, such as in anticipatory anxiety or a panic attack.

What Does This Mean in the Classroom?

The student needs to feel safe within the classroom and know that the teacher will not embarrass her in front of peers. Speaking privately to the student about what helps calm them will assist in meeting those needs. Some students need a safe place within the classroom or within the school where they can go to calm down; others may need a special item, such as a fidget or a toy, that they can carry when they are feeling anxious.

Anticipatory Anxiety or Grief

Anticipatory anxiety is considered a main feature of social anxiety disorder. Problems with emotional regulation are linked to social anxiety disorder. Because children anticipate something bad happening in the future, they may avoid social situations (Helbig-Lang, Rusch, Rief, & Lincoln, 2015). If a child is bitten by a dog, every time the child sees a dog, she may anticipate getting bitten.

A characteristic of social anxiety is rumination, meaning to ponder or think about something over and over. When an event has happened, the child will focus on the negative aspects of the event over and over, and not the positive ones. This process of rumination makes the event seem more negative than it was; the child anticipates something terrible happening at the next social event. Individuals who greatly fear getting a negative evaluation in a social situation maintain a negative perception of their performance and have a negative memory bias (Einsel & Turk, 2011).

Anticipatory anxiety can occur well in advance of upcoming situations. The child may then avoid the feared social situations (American Psychiatric Association, 2013).

As children face many life crises, like the anticipated death of a parent due to illness or their own anticipated death by a progressive disease, professionals are increasingly studying anticipatory anxiety or grief. When the child learns that a parent is ill and may die, the child can exhibit a range of issues from absenteeism, withdrawal, anxiety, social problems, and fright. If one family member has died, the child may fear that another member of the family will also die.

What Does This Mean in the Classroom?

When a parent is ill, the child will need additional support; the educator will need to engage in active listening and understanding.

Structure and routine at school are important because of changes in routine that occur at home due to the parent's illness. If there is going to be a known change in the schedule, the student should be told about it in advance.

Children can be taught positive self-talk as they cope during a difficult time (Hearst, 2009). School can be a safe place where the child is given some control, such as a choice between two as-signments, a choice of where to work, and a choice of with whom to work.

Separation Anxiety Disorder

Separation anxiety disorder occurs when a child engages in inappropriate and excessive fear when separated from an individual with whom the child is attached. This is characterized by at least three of the following: recurring distress that is excessive when either anticipating or experiencing separation from major attachment figures; excessive worry about losing attachment figures; excessive worry about experiencing an untoward event, reluctance, or refusal to go out; excessive reluctance about being alone; reluctance or refusal to sleep away from home or go to sleep without being near the person she is close to; repeated nightmares about separations; and repeated physical complaints (American Psychiatric Association, 2013).

The question is: Is it an age-inappropriate irrational fear of being separated from a caregiver? When forced to separate, the child may exhibit extreme distress, throw tantrums, or report being ill (Swan, Cummings, Caporino, & Kendall, 2014).

Separation anxiety is diagnosed in children and adolescents if it persists for four weeks or more and causes significant distress or impairment in academic, social, or other areas of functioning (American Psychiatric Association, 2013).

What Does This Mean in the Classroom?

Teaching relaxation strategies to students such as progressive muscle relaxation and deep breathing can be helpful, as well as teaching self-talk strategies. Reductions in negative self-talk can impact the child's behaviors and emotions. Children can learn to recognize their own patterns of anxious thinking and learn positive ways to control such thinking (Swan, Cummings, Caporino, & Kendall, 2014).

Selective Mutism

Selective mutism is a consistent failure to speak in social situations where it is expected that the individual will speak, and yet the individual can speak in other situations. Selective mutism is diagnosed if it interferes with educational achievement or with social skills and the duration is at least one month, excluding the first month of school. Selective mutism is not explained by a communication disorder; children with selective mutism have already established the capacity to speak in some situations (American Psychiatric Association, 2013).

A teacher reported that one of her second-grade students had not spoken in class all year. After contacting the parent, the teacher learned that the child had not spoken in class any year, nor does the child speak to anyone except her parents and siblings. Even the grandparents have had little success in getting the child to speak. Doctors have found nothing to explain the mutism. This information should have been conveyed to the teacher before the beginning of the school year. The child seems to be doing well academically, earning passing grades, but often seems sad and isolated in class. Pressure to speak can cause undue stress on the child.

What Does This Mean in the Classroom?

Getting a child to feel comfortable in class can begin by establishing trust in the teacher. This may be established non-verbally first, giving the child time to react and respond. Make eye contact with all students while exhibiting a pleasant facial expression. Look at any other student, point to a foam ball, and gently roll the ball across the student's desktop. Without words, indicate to this student to gently return the foam ball. When the student returns it, smile and nod your head. This models expectations of this easy fun activity to all students. Repeat the activity by rolling the ball to other students. Continue passing the ball back and forth silently until the student who does not speak feels comfortable and then roll it to them. Show your praise and acceptance non-verbally by smiling and nodding your head. Before the student realizes it, they are engaged, communicating, and having fun! Then go on with the lesson for that period. The next day, try a similar activity. The teacher can also ask them to draw, write, or pantomime to communicate. Eventually, the student becomes engaged and comfortable, interested in class, and trusting. Avoid putting the student on the spot by calling on the student in front of the entire class. Try going to their desk to demonstrate part of the lesson, talk softly to the student, and eventually start to engage them in communication by asking open-ended questions.

Generalized Anxiety Disorders

Generalized anxiety disorders are characterized by excessive anxiety and worry, occurring for at least six months, and are associated with events or activities such as work or school performance. Only one of these characteristics is required for the diagnosis of a child: restlessness or feeling on edge, easily fatigued, difficulty concentrating, irritability, muscle tension, or sleep disturbance (American Psychiatric Association, 2013). These disorders can include academic anxiety, test anxiety, and overachieving, which can become a generalized anxiety disorder if seen in the extreme for at least six months.

What Does This Mean in the Classroom?

Effective interventions have been studied for children in grades K to 12. The most effective are those that have their basis in cognitive or behavioral therapy. They combine strategies such as relaxation techniques, slow exposure to tasks causing anxiety, and positive recognition for coping strategies. Security tools may be needed for the student; these can be fidgets or special toys that are small and can be carried by the child.

Academic Anxiety

It has been found that high academic anxiety is detrimental to achievement, but moderate levels of academic anxiety are associated with higher achievement (Gillen-O'Neel, Ruble, & Fuligni, 2011; see also, El-Anzi, 2005; Sharma, 1970).

There is a link between high levels of anxiety and impaired cognitive performance, resulting in poor academic outcomes. The student may have difficulty concentrating and recalling earlier academic knowledge. When students are anxious about their school performance, a reduction in anxiety can lead to better engagement with academic tasks (Wood, 2007). Some students with anxiety disorders develop learned-helplessness where they avoid tasks they believe are too difficult for them. Students give up easily and withdraw from the tasks (Killu & Crundwell, 2016).

Gillen-O'Neel, Ruble, and Fuligni (2011) studied ethnic stigma and academic anxiety. Those individuals from ethnic-minority backgrounds are frequently stigmatized and may face increased risk for negative academic outcomes. Regardless of the specific ethnic group, perception of group status and peer regard was associated with academic anxiety.

While it is known that anxiety can result in academic underachievement, what impact do certain academic tasks have on increasing anxiety? Carey, Devine, Hill, and Szucs (2017) studied math anxiety, test anxiety, and generalized anxiety. Girls with academic anxieties may develop it because of a general predisposition to anxiety, while boys develop high levels of academic anxiety without such a predisposition. Girls have a higher level of anxiety in academics, while boys are found to have higher test and math anxieties.

Academic buoyancy is a term used by some authors (Putwain, Daly, Chamberlain, & Sadreddini, 2015). It is defined as the ability to withstand the routine setbacks, pressures, and challenges experienced throughout a student's educational career. Academic buoyancy is positively related to lower general academic anxiety. Students who are academically buoyant protect themselves from any negative appraisal of performance by drawing on their positive self-beliefs, effort, and motivation. Students who show greater academic anxiety tend to be less academically buoyant.

What Does This Mean in the Classroom?

It is important for educators to give relevant and helpful feedback to students after they complete academic tasks. Rather than focusing on what the student got wrong which will probably increase that student's anxiety, educators should point out what was done well and then what can be improved. Creating scoring rubrics so students know exactly what the teacher is looking for in grading are very helpful.

Simple strategies such as having students identify and record their strengths can increase a student's capacity to become academically buoyant. It is also important to teach students to attribute their success to controllable factors, such as effort and utilizing strategies, and to teach students to control their thought distortions that might result in panic (Putwain, Daly, Chamberlain, & Sadreddini, 2015).

Test Anxiety

By increasing a student's academic buoyancy, they will perform better on tests. Because of the widespread use of high-stakes testing, educators are focusing more than ever on the reality of test anxiety. Test anxiety is defined as the emotional, physiological, and behavioral responses that surround the possible consequences of negative test scores (Von Der Embse, Barterian, & Segool, 2013). Anxious feeling and thoughts and off-task behaviors interfere in testing situations. Individuals who are test anxious worry about failure, criticize themselves, compare themselves to others, and are distracted. Anxiety decreases academic performance. Worry is considered the most powerful component of test anxiety (Eum & Rice, 2011; Zeidner, 1998).

What Does This Mean in the Classroom?

As in generalized anxiety disorder, cognitive or behavioral theory is most effective in the reduction of test anxiety. Relaxation techniques, such as having the student close their eyes for 45 seconds and think of something that makes them happy before beginning a test, can be effective. Positive self-talk can also be effective.

Test-taking strategies, such as how to take a multiple choice test, how to find keywords that suggest that an answer is probably wrong, and teaching students how to read the direction on tests, have been found to be effective.

Meeting the sensory needs of the student during testing is helpful. Does the student need to be able to play with a fidget? Does the student need to have a water bottle? On testing days, is the student wearing comfortable clothes?

Systematic desensitization has also been found to be effective. Such strategies involve the use of relaxation techniques during exposure to a feared test (Von Der Embse, Barterian, & Segool, 2013).

Biofeedback is an intervention using self-monitoring devices for physiological purposes such as monitoring heart rate, muscle tension, and body temperature (Von Der Embse, Barterian, & Segool, 2013).

Academic interventions help students prepare for tests. When students are having difficulty with vocabulary, the teacher can teach the required vocabulary. Skill-building interventions are needed in preparing for tests. Assessing the student's weaknesses and teaching those skills will result in the student being better prepared.

Overachievers

A growing population of students have become obsessed with getting grades good enough to get into prestigious universities. These students deal with illnesses or physical deterioration, such as losing their hair. They may cheat to get better test results or engage in buying papers from other students. Their parents may be obsessed and pressure their children to be the best, at any cost (Robbins, 2006).

Students who have high performance expectations and low levels of negative self-evaluation can be described as possessing adaptive perfectionism. Students with adaptive perfectionism have approach-goals rather than avoidance-goals and believe in mastery over performance. They exhibit more intrinsic than extrinsic motivation (Eum & Rice, 2011).

Maladaptive perfectionism is described as having high performance expectations and high levels of self-blame if they do not meet their own set standards. Students with maladaptive perfectionism have goals that indicate their fear of failure and doubts about their adequacy in mastering material. These students exhibited cognitive test anxiety. They were also more concerned with making good impressions in performance situations and not betraying their inadequacies (Eum & Rice, 2011).

Some have described over-achievement as an addiction. It can be a combination of workaholism, perfectionism, and competitiveness. The unhealthy overachiever collects or is pushed to collect goals for the sake of collecting them (Robbins, 2006).

What Does This Mean in the Classroom?

Particularly during middle and secondary school years, it is important for educators to coordinate the scheduling of testing so that students are not bombarded with too many tests on one day. This prevents students from becoming overwhelmed when studying for tests and allows them to better manage their time for studying.

Schools can also increase the number of less competitive alternatives for students. The more competition students face, the more they become anxious. Robbins (2006) suggests recreational sports leagues or one act plays.

Teaching students mindfulness activities and time management may also assist. Educators must look for early warning signs that students are becoming stressed because of too many demands to overachieve.

TEN TEACHING TIPS

1. When providing feedback to students with anxiety disorders, focus on what was done correctly and then provide constructive feedback to improve what was not done well.
2. Scoring rubrics should be provided to students, so they know exactly how an assignment will be graded.
3. Teach students to focus on their strengths.
4. Teach students to attribute their successes to their efforts.
5. Teach students relaxation strategies; deep breathing can be effective to students with anxiety disorders.
6. Teachers should model positive self-talk with their students and teach their students to engage in such talk.
7. Teachers should be very careful to use a calm and caring approach that refrains from embarrassing the student in front of peers.
8. Provide identified tools that will calm the student such as a safe area within the classroom or in another part of the building, or a special item such as a fidget or a toy that can be carried.
9. Avoid surprises in the classroom and provide structure and routine.
10. Plan ahead for any activities that might result in anxiety for the student and make a contingency plan to ensure that the student is treated with respect and dignity and is not put into an embarrassing or anxiety-provoking situation.

Creative Connections
I can't . . . but I CAN—Elementary or Secondary

How individuals perceive the events in their lives can affect how others respond to them. Everybody has good days and bad days. Children who experience anxiety often have negative thoughts that can contribute to stress and anxiety. Positive outlook can increase our enjoyment of daily life and decrease anxiety. This creative activity identifies things we cannot do, but quickly changes the focus to all the things we CAN do! Then, students create visual, literary, or performing arts to articulate and celebrate all the things "I CAN do"! This shifts the emphasis from the negative to the positive.

Create

Begin by asking students to write a list of all the things they cannot do. Give examples, such as "I cannot play a musical instrument," "I cannot drive a car," and "I cannot run a marathon." Then have the students make a different list with all the things they CAN do. This list is usually shorter and more difficult to compile, so challenge them to make a long list with at least 20 things they can do. It is human nature to be hard on ourselves and to have a difficult time listing all the things we can do. Give students a few minutes to make their lists, then have them share with a person sitting next to them. If another student shares something that is applicable to the first student but that student did not think to list, they have permission to add that to their own list. The facilitator/teacher can also give examples to stimulate ideas for the lists: I can listen when someone needs to talk, I can be patient, I can laugh at silly things, I can feel the warmth of the sun, I can hear rain on a rainy day, I can call a friend when I am bored, I can color outside the lines, I can jump rope, and so on. This project can be adapted to any student age range. For younger students, have them state rather than write their lists.

Give students choices in creatively communicating things they can do. For example, students can write a poem, perform a skit or rap, or draw pictures. Another idea is to create an "I CAN" book. On each page, have students draw or glue pictures cut out from magazines, or write a sentence or paragraph to fill the pages in their book.

Reflect

After students create, have them share their creations with the class. Ask them to reflect on the process and to reflect on their attitude toward all the things they can do. Did this activity add to the ideas of things you can do? Did it help to change your focus from the things you cannot do to the many things you can do? Did it transform negative thoughts to the positive? Next time you feel stress or worry increasing, are there things you focused on today that can help you maintain a positive attitude?

Peace Box or Calm Kit—Elementary Level

Having a box with a variety of small sensory items for children to choose from can help kids begin to self-manage and self-soothe as they work toward independence. Giving them choices is important. This box of items becomes a variety of tools for them to select when they feel stress beginning to take over. It is a non-threatening, creative way to give them strategies and develop confidence to be able to manage their own anxiety.

Assemble a box of purchased items or make the box specific to your student(s). Ask the child, "What comforts you in times of stress?" Note that initially they may not be able to answer that question, but it is important to get their ideas first and then make suggestions to add to their list of tools. Using a cardboard box, canvas bag, or a basket, let the student decorate and label the box. Begin to assemble things for the box with the suggested items.

Suggested Items to Include in the Peace Box or Calm Kit

Small mirror to practice relaxing their face
Blank paper and crayons or markers for coloring
Sound therapy—an iPod or CD player with earbuds for listening to calming music
Photo of a special place: beach, their backyard, and mountains
Stuffed animal
Warm soft socks
Soft piece of fabric

Kaleidoscope

Neck roll—soft pillow, rolled towel, or a travel neck pillow to hug the neck

Laminated cards with instructions guiding them to hum a song, drink water, draw a picture, and count slowly, or whisper the alphabet

Envelopes with pen and blank cards and the instructions: Write what you are feeling, and put it in an envelope

Stress balls—instructions for making stress balls follow

Stress Balls

Having the students make their own stress balls can be empowering. They can make one for the peace box or calm kit, and they can make one to keep at their desk. Give students choices when possible, for example, use balloons in a variety of colors and markers for students to draw on the balloons if they choose.

Materials

Different colors of balloons
Flour
Spoons or scoops
Funnels
Markers for decorating the balloon

Directions

Allow the students to pick the color of balloon. Place the funnel in the mouth of the balloon. Demonstrate how to scoop the flour into the funnel and gently tap until the flour fills the balloon. Take care not to over fill the balloon. Knot the end of the balloon. Give students a choice of decorating their balloon or writing their name on their balloon with markers (do not use pencils or pens).

This stress ball is soft, easy to manipulate, and very soothing for young and old.

KEY TAKEAWAYS

♦ Individuals with social anxiety disorder experience difficulties in utilizing emotional regulation strategies for dealing with anticipatory anxiety.

♦ Students who show greater academic anxiety tend to be less academically buoyant.

♦ Students exhibiting maladaptive perfectionism fear failure, have doubts about their ability to master material, and exhibit cognitive test anxiety.

♦ Cognitive and behavioral therapy have been found to be effective in the treatment of generalized anxiety disorders. PTSDs are triggered by external events. Other anxiety disorders may be caused by internal conflicts within the individual.

REFERENCES

American Psychiatric Association. (2013). *Diagnostic and statistical manual of mental disorders* (5th ed.). Washington, DC: American Psychiatric Publishing.

Carey, E., Devine, A., Hill, F., & Szucs, D. (2017). Differentiating anxiety forms and their role in academic performance from primary to secondary school. *PLoS ONE, 12(3)*, E0174418. doi:10.1371journal.pone.0174418

Einsel, K., & Turk, C. (2011). Social anxiety and rumination: Effect on anticipatory anxiety, memory bias, and beliefs. *Psi Chi Journal of Undergraduate Research, 16(1)*, 26–31.

El-Anzi, F. (2005). Academic achievement and its relationship with anxiety, self-esteem, optimism, and pessimism in Kuwaiti students. *Social Behavior and Personality, 33*, 95–104.

Eum, K., & Rice, K. (2011). Test anxiety, perfectionism, goal orientation, and academic performance. *Anxiety, Stress, and Coping, 24(2)*, 167–178.

Fletcher, K. (2011). Understanding and assessing traumatic responses of guilt, shame, and anger among children, adolescents, and young adults. *Journal of Child and Adolescent Trauma, 4*, 339–360.

Gillen-O'Neel, C., Ruble, D., & Fuligni, A. (2011). Ethnic stigma, academic anxiety, and intrinsic motivation in middle childhood. *Child Development, 82(5)*, 1470–1485.

Gutermann, J., Schreiber, F., Matulis, S., Schwartzkopff, L., Deppe, J., & Steil, R. (2016). Psychological treatments for symptoms of posttraumatic stress disorder in children, adolescents, and young adults: A meta-analysis. *Clinical Child and Family Psychology Review, 19*, 77–93.

Hearst, D. (2009). The runaway child: Managing anticipatory fear, resistance and distress in children undergoing surgery. *Pediatric Anesthesia, 19*, 1014–1016.

Helbig-Lang, S., Rusch, S., Rief, W., & Lincoln, T. (2015). The strategy does not matter: Effects of acceptance, reappraisal, and distraction on the course of anticipatory anxiety in social anxiety disorder. *Psychology and Psychotherapy: Theory, Research, and Practice, 88*, 366–377.

Killu, K., & Crundwell, R. (2016). Students with anxiety in the classroom: Educational accommodations and interventions. *Beyond Behavior, 25(2)*, 30–40.

Putwain, D., Daly, A., Chamberlain, S., & Sadreddini, S. (2015). Academically buoyant students are less anxious about and perform better in high-stakes examinations. *British Journal of Educational Psychology, 85*, 247–263.

Robbins, A. (2006). *The overachievers: The secret lives of driven kids.* New York, NY: Hachette Books.

Sharma, S. (1970). Manifest anxiety and school achievement of adolescents. *Journal of Consulting and Clinical Psychology, 34*, 403–407.

Steele, W., & Kuban, C. (2014). Healing trauma, building resilience: SITCAP in action. *Reclaiming Children and Youth, 22(4)*, 18–20.

Swan, A., Cummings, C., Caporino, N., & Kendall, P. (2014). Evidence-based intervention approaches for students with anxiety and related disorders. In H. Walker & F. Gresham (Eds.), *Handbook of evidence-based practices for emotional and behavioral disorders* (pp. 324–343). New York, NY: Guilford Press.

Von Der Embse, N., Barterian, J., & Segool, N. (2013). Test anxiety interventions for children and adolescents: A systematic review of treatment studies from 2000–2010. *Psychology in the Schools, 50(1)*, 57–71.

Wood, J. (2007). Effect of anxiety reduction on children's school performance and social adjustment. *Developmental Psychology, 42(2)*, 345–349.

Zeidner, M. (1998). *Test anxiety. The state of the art.* New York, NY: Plenum.

3

Causes of Anxiety Disorders

THIS STRESSES ME OUT!!!!! I wish I knew why but I just don't. Sometimes my anxiety wins.

Girl, Age 10

LIVE FROM THE CLASSROOM

Mrs. Huntington and Mrs. Brown commute together to their teaching jobs in a middle school with a diverse population of students. About half of their students are eligible for free or reduced meals. Mrs. Huntington is very frustrated. Two of her students who have social anxiety disorder had a melt-down during a confrontation with another student. A third student became frustrated when he had to take a test, started crying and had to leave the room. Mrs. Huntington is trying to figure out what is causing her students' anxiety. Mrs. Brown comments, "I think it's just coming from their homes. I blame their parents." Mrs. Huntington answers, "I just don't feel it's that simple, but I don't know what is causing their anxiety."

Introduction to Causes of Anxiety

What Causes Anxiety Disorders?

Many educators perceive that there is an increase in students exhibiting anxiety. This chapter discusses the causes of anxiety. It may never be known what caused one child to have an anxiety disorder and another child not to, even when they have had similar experiences or are from the same family. Causes have to be viewed as possibilities or probabilities because it can seldom be decided that a certain event or occurrence caused a given problem. Some children are more vulnerable than others; a variety of causes may work together, and thus, the subject can become very complex (Kauffman & Badar, 2018).

Causes of Anxiety

Genetics

Genetics partly determine each individual. Someone may be genetically predisposed to certain conditions: Some families have a history of heart problems, cancer, or a specific disease. Certain mental health issues can also be predisposed. The causes of anxiety and depression are not known, but it has been found that a complex interaction between genetic susceptibility and environmental factors is the main cause (Spruyt, 2016). Separation anxiety can occur with having a history of a distressing separation experience and be based on a neurobiological determined vulnerability. Vulnerability or resilience to traumatic stress appears to be determined by genetic and neurobiological factors (Bandelow et al., 2016).

Childhood obsessive-compulsive disorder (OCD) is considered a highly familial disorder, but there are few genetic studies (Do Rosario-Campos et al., 2005). Genetic research has changed the view of the cause of anxiety disorders, OCD, and post-traumatic stress disorder (PTSD). Previously, it was thought that childhood adversities, rearing styles, or negative parental attitudes were responsible. However, heritability estimates for anxiety disorders, OCD, and PTSD have been found to range on an average of 50%, which leaves the remaining half for an interaction of environmental factors, such as adversities, stressors, substance abuse, and many others. Unfortunately, genetic research has not identified the genes that are definitely associated with any one of the disorders (Bandelow et al., 2016).

In a study of six-year-old twins, it was estimated that when a parent had experienced separation anxiety, 73% of those studied were found to have it. There was an even higher rate in females. In social anxiety when a first-degree relative had such disorder, the relatives had a two to six times greater chance of having the same disorder. For children with generalized anxiety disorder, one-third of the cause has been found to be genetic. For OCD, having a first-degree relative with onset of OCD as a child increased the likelihood of inheritance by 10 times (American Psychiatric Association, 2013).

Biological Markers

Biomarkers can be defined as anatomical, biochemical, or physiological traits that an individual possesses. There is no test or imaging method to diagnose anxiety disorders, OCD, or PTSD. Studies of the neurobiology of mental disorders are usually based on comparisons between those who are impacted by anxiety, OCD, or PTSD versus those who are part of a healthy control groups (Bandelow et al., 2016).

Psychosocial Stressors

Psychosocial stressors associated with anxiety disorders include traumatic experiences during childhood or adolescence, death of a parent, separation from parents, family marital discord, childhood illness, sexual or physical violence, or a family history of mental illness (Bandelow et al., 2017).

Temperament

The child's temperament or internal traits can impact the likelihood of specific anxiety disorders. In specific phobias, children show a temperament with negative affectivity, also called neuroticism or behavioral inhibition. Children with social anxiety disorders are predisposed with the characteristics of behavioral inhibition and fear of negative evaluation. In generalized anxiety disorders, children have indicators of behavioral inhibition, neuroticism, and harm avoidance. For children with OCD, there is higher negative emotionality and behavioral inhibitions (American Psychiatric Association, 2013).

Behavioral inhibitions are defined as a consistent tendency to show fear, uncertainty, or withdrawal when the child face new situations. Fearful temperaments involve negative affectivity, which is characterized by negative moods, difficulty in being soothed, and irritability. Infant and toddler research has consistently linked this to later inhibition and anxiety (Affrunti & Woodruff-Borden, 2015; Rapee & Coplan, 2010).

Temperamental risk factors in selective mutism are not well defined, but the children may have subtle language difficulties. For children who have a hoarding disorder, indecisiveness is a prominent feature (American Psychiatric Association, 2013).

Environmental Causes

Some have argued that specific parenting styles and family functioning cause child anxiety, but this has not been supported in research. However, Jongerden and Bogels (2015) have found that good relational functioning is associated with better long-term outcomes for adolescents. Families of children who were referred for anxiety did not differ from families of control children with regard to anxiety-enhancing parenting. Children who exhibit selective mutism may model their parents' social inhibition. Parents of these children tend to be overprotective and more controlling than parents of children with other anxiety disorders (American Psychiatric Association, 2013). Physical and sexual abuse and other stressful events in a child's life are associated with an increased risk for OCD. Educators cannot assume that all children with OCD have experienced such abuse.

Environmental factors in PTSD include lower socioeconomic status, racial/ethnic status, and other instances of childhood adversity with exposure to prior trauma (American Psychiatric Association, 2013).

Brain Chemistry

Brain imaging studies have shown that abnormalities within orbitofrontal-basal ganglia neural circuits represent an important feature of OCD. In OCD, structural changes are found throughout the entire brain. A comparison of OCD, panic disorders, and PTSD showed decreased bilateral gray-matter volumes in dorsomedial and anterior cingulate gyri across all three disorders (Bandelow et al., 2017). Children with OCD had higher levels of right prefrontal white-matter choline and N-acetyl aspartate (NAA) (Weber et al., 2014). White matter integrity was compromised in some brain regions of children with OCD (Rosso et al., 2014).

Research in functional imaging has found greater activity in the amygdala and insula in PTSD, social anxiety disorder, and specific phobia, but the greatest activity is in social anxiety disorder and specific phobia.

Medical Conditions

Some medical conditions increase the risk of anxiety and depression. There is a hypothesis that one OCD subtype is associated with autoimmune disorders triggered by streptococcal infections. Children who develop acute OCD after such an infection were described by Swedo (2002), who coined the PANDAS (pediatric autoimmune neuropsychiatric disorders associated with streptococcal infections). Many children get a streptococcal infection without developing PANDAS, so a genetic vulnerability may be necessary. In children with panic disorder, an association with respiratory disturbance such as asthma has been found (American Psychiatric Association, 2013).

Stress Triggers

Not all stress is negative: It can help people to get moving and get things done. There are three different types of stress: positive stress, tolerable stress, and toxic stress. Positive stress is mild to moderate stress that is handled well by the child, especially when a responsive adult provides coping assistance. Tolerable stress is more threatening than positive stress, so it involves a higher level of physiological response: If the child has access to strong protective adult relationships, the child can return to a healthy state. Toxic stress is chronic and cannot be mediated, even by a strong responsive adult: Brain and body development is altered in ways that impair future life functioning, and the number of neurons in the brain are altered (Shonkoff et al., 2012; see also, Patterson & Vakili, 2014). Chronic exposure to stress in young children, including deprivation of relationships, primes the brain to be more responsive to stress throughout life (Patterson & Vakili, 2014).

Risk of suicide in panic disorders increases when comorbid with depression (Spruyt, 2016).

Gender Issues

Females have a higher rate of anxiety disorders. The female-to-male ratio of the prevalence rates of anxiety disorders varies between 1.5:1 and 2.1:1. Psychosocial factors such as childhood sexual abuse, chronic stressors, gender discrimination, and genetic and neurobiological factors have been discussed as possible reasons. It is likely that female sex hormones are involved and that the gender-specific risk is a genetic one (Bandelow et al., 2017).

Poverty

Living in poverty has many negative effects on children's physical and mental health. These children who are more likely to live in substandard housing, be exposed to more danger, have poor nutrition, inadequate child care, and lack access to health care have a higher risk of mental health problems (Gupta, 2017). The effects of poverty on implicit emotional reactivity in the amygdala are mostly seen in females. In males, the effects of poverty result in impaired function of the emotional regulatory regions of the brain (Javanbakht et al., 2016).

Mental illness in children is attributed to risk factors that are associated with poverty. Adults with adverse childhood experiences, such as growing up in poverty, may raise their children in environments that provide toxic stress. This can become an intergenerational cycle of mental health disorders (Patterson & Vakili, 2014).

Grief and Loss

Bereavement, grief, and mourning are three different terms in the literature. Bereavement refers to the objective experience of having a loved one die, grief is the reaction to the bereavement, and mourning is defined as cultural practices in expressing grief.

There is normal and pathological grief. Children who suffer from childhood traumatic grief perceive the death as traumatic, are overwhelmed, and cannot engage in the normal grieving process. When compared to youth who have been exposed to trauma without death, the bereaved trauma survivors report higher levels of PTSD symptoms, arousal, worry, depression, and physical health complaints (Brown & Goodman, 2005).

Brown and Goodman (2005) found that communicating about and remembering the person who died were helpful strategies for children who experienced trauma on September 11, 2001. Bergman, Axberg, and Hanson (2017) reviewed 17 studies about children who had lost a parent. Of concern was the bereavement research showing the vulnerability of young children because of their dependence on their caregiver.

What Can Be Learned from the Research?

Since there are many possible causes of anxiety disorders, educators should not judge or blame. The issues are complex in that there is no definitive cause and no quick fix for students who have anxiety disorders. Educators do not need to know the cause in order to understand and lend support to the student (Sink & Igelman, 2004).

Research conducted with children in urban, high poverty areas has suggested that promotive facts such as self-efficacy and positive expectations about the future can yield positive outcomes for students. Children who reported more positive expectations reported lower levels of symptoms of anxiety and depression (O'Neal & Cotton, 2016). Educators have the potential to positively affect children and may reduce symptoms of anxiety by communicating positive expectations.

Providing social support to students has been found to be a protective factor to a traumatic event exposure.

TEN TEACHING TIPS

1. Find ways to support parents of children who have anxiety disorders.
2. Refrain from judgment or blame of parents.

3. Initiate and maintain ongoing dialogue with parents and school social workers to explore effective strategies for helping children.
4. Educators can be the responsive adults who provide coping strategies when students are stressed.
5. Every child is different, and therefore, a strategy that works for one child may not work for another.
6. Let students know that they can succeed.
7. Provide recognition for students for small accomplishments.
8. Model positive thinking.
9. To foster independence and teach decision-making, provide choices throughout the day.
10. Network with other agencies to provide basic needs for students.

Creative Connections

The Same but Different

Everyone has trouble making decisions at one time or another, but for some students, making the "right" decision can be traumatic, even immobilizing. Art provides opportunities for making decisions in which there is no right or wrong choice, but rather a variety of options, some of which will work better than others specifically for the person making the choice.

In "The Same but Different" project, every student receives the same materials with which to work, but then chooses how they will use these materials to create a work of art. It is expected that some students will choose to create a two-dimensional project, some will create in three-dimension, and others will decide to work in a combination of both (bas-relief). Each student is given a paper bag containing the same materials. Additionally, "group materials," such as tape, glue, staplers, markers, and paint, may be available for everyone in the class to use. This project can be done with any age group, from pre-K to 12, using age-appropriate materials and time allotments.

Materials

Be creative and age appropriate in what is chosen, but be consistent so that all the bags have the exact same contents. Some examples of materials to be put in the bag are pipe cleaners; note cards; aluminum foil; plastic wrap; wax paper; newspaper; tissue paper; bubble wrap; textured fabric such as velvet, silk, satin, faux fur, or burlap; wooden clothes pins; wooden popsicle sticks; similarly shaped blocks of wood; similar tree branches; a length of string or yarn; beans, peas or rice; empty plastic bottles; bottle caps both plastic and metal; sea shells; and plastic flowers.

Directions

Explain that each student will be given a bag of supplies to use to make an art project. Let the students know that you expect every project to be different and that you look forward to seeing all the different projects that can be made using the same materials. Tell the students that they are not required to use all the supplies in the bag and may also use the "group materials." Give each student a preassembled bag containing the materials to be used. Remind the students to find a place on their art project to put their name. When the projects are completed, place all of the projects on a table and allow the students an opportunity to walk around and look at everyone's project. A discussion might be held addressing the differences of each project. The students may also discuss what was the most fun part of the project, what was easy about the project, what was challenging, what they think turned out the best on their project, and what they would change if they had a chance to re-do the project. If possible, display the projects with signage explaining the parameters of the project.

OPEN MIC—Secondary Students

This creative activity is non-threatening, allowing everyone to participate, including all students with no prior experience with art. The goal is to facilitate a process so that students will recognize success as they share positive responses to works of art.

Materials

One art image for every student in class: Art images can be on a digital slideshow or printed posters. Number the images

1–30 (or the total number of students in one class); strips of paper numbered 1 through however many students are in that class; bag or hat from which to draw a number; cardboard rolls, such as a paper towel roll; and construction paper to make a microphone or talking stick.

Directions

Each student will assemble a microphone or talking stick using a cardboard roll and construction paper.

Students select a number to indicate which art image they will evaluate. Explain that all art has at least one quality that is successful, and most art has at least one characteristic that could be improved to make it even better. Students will select a number from the hat and focus on the corresponding work of art to determine and share one successful aspect, and something that might have made it even more successful. The students will use their mics to voice their opinions. Students must justify their responses: They cannot just say, "I like it," or "I don't like it," but must tell at least one thing the artist did that makes it successful and one way in which it could have been improved.

To help students with vocabulary, make two lists of examples on the board, one for positive critiques and one for negative art criticism. The first might include good composition, excellent workmanship, good use of color, expressive line quality, strong focal point, intriguing—makes me want to talk to the artist, nice variety of shapes, placement of color creates movement, placement of shapes creates energy, tells a story, interesting texture, at least three values, color intensity is effective, nice repetition, it evokes a personal memory, and it inspires me to make art.

A vocabulary bank for suggestions for improving the art can include the artist could have used brighter colors to make it more cheerful, added something in this empty space to make it more interesting, improve workmanship, add a variety of shapes to make it more interesting, limited shapes to make it more cohesive, limit the colors to make it less confusing, the artist might have improved the quality of the design by showing artistic skill, this work of art makes me feel sad, or it makes me feel nervous.

Variation

Instead of art images, have students respond to different music genres, such as rap, jazz, orchestral, country, pop, rock, hillbilly, and blues.

Create two vocabulary banks of sample responses pertaining to music, successful and ways it might be improved.

KEY TAKEAWAYS

♦ Children who live in poverty are at a higher risk of anxiety disorders.

♦ Approximately 50% of the causes of anxiety disorders can be genetically linked.

♦ Exposures to high levels of toxic stress can cause lasting problems in life functioning.

♦ Causes of anxiety disorders are complex.

♦ Educators can initiate strategies that help children experiencing anxiety without knowing the definitive cause.

REFERENCES

Affrunti, N., & Woodruff-Borden, J. (2015). The associations of executive function and temperament in a model of risk for childhood anxiety. *Journal of Child and Family Studies, 24,* 715–724.

American Psychiatric Association. (2013). *Diagnostic and statistical manual of mental disorders* (5th ed.). Washington, DC: American Psychiatric Association.

Bandelow, B., Baldwin, D., Abelli, M., Altamura, C., Dell'Osso, B., Domschke, K., Fineberg, N. Grunblatt, E., Jarema, M., Maron, E., Nutt, D., Pini, S. Vaghi, M., Wichniak, A., Zai, G., & Riederer, P. (2016). Biological markers for anxiety disorders, OCD, and PTSD—A consensus statement. Part I: Neuroimaging and genetics. *The World Journal of Biological Psychiatry, 17(5),* 321–365.

Bandelow, B., Baldwin, D., Abelli, M., Bolea-Alamanac, B., Bourin, M., Chamberlain, S., Cinosi, E., Davies, S., Domschke, K., Fineberg, N., Grunblatt, E., Jarema, M., Kim, Y, Maron, E., Masdrakis, V., Mikova, O., Nutt, D., Pallanti, S., Pini, S., Strohle, A., Thibaut, F., Vaghi, M., Won, E., Wedekind, D., Wichniak, A., Wooley, J., Zwanzger, P., & Riederer, P. (2017). Biological markers for anxiety disorders, OCD and PTSD—A consensus statement. Part II: Neurochemistry, neurophysiology, and neurocognition. *The World Journal of Biological Psychiatry, 18(3)*, 162–214.

Bergman, A., Axberg, U., & Hanson, E. (2017). When a parent dies—A systematic review of the effects of support programs for parentally bereaved children and their caregivers. *BMC Palliative Care, 16(39)*, 1–15.

Brown, E., & Goodman, R. (2005). Childhood traumatic grief: An exploration of the construct in children bereaved on September 11. *Journal of Clinical Child and Adolescent Psychology, 34(2)*, 248–259.

Do Rosario-Campos, M., Leckman, J., Curi, M., Quatrano, S., Katsovitch, L., Miguel, E., & Pauls, D. (2005). A family study of early-onset obsessive-compulsive disorder. *American Journal of Medical Genetics B Neuropsychiatric Genetics, 136B*, 92–97.

Gupta, D. (2017). UN-employment, poverty and recession impact on youth's mental health. *Indian Journal of Health and Well-being, 8(8)*, 911–914.

Javanbakht, A., Kim, P., Swain, J., Evans, G., Phan, L., & Liberzon, I. (2016). Sex-specific effects of childhood poverty on neuro-circuitry of processing of emotional cues: A neuroimaging study. *Behavioral Sciences, 6(28)*, 1–11.

Jongerden, L., & Bogels, S. (2015). Parenting, family functioning and anxiety-disordered children: comparisons to controls, changes after family versus child CBT. *Journal of Child and Family Studies, 24*, 2046–2059.

Kauffman, J., & Badar, J. (2018). *The scandalous neglect of children's mental health: What schools can do.* New York, NY: Routledge.

O'Neal, L., & Cotton, S. (2016). Promotive factors and psychosocial adjustment among urban youth. *Child and Youth Care Forum, 45*, 947–961.

Patterson, J., & Vakili, S. (2014). Relationships, environment, and the brain: How emerging research is changing what we know about the impact of families on human development. *Family Process, 53(1)*, 22–32.

Rapee, R., & Coplan, R. (2010). Conceptual relations between anxiety disorder and fearful temperament. In H. Gazelle & K. H. Rubin (Eds.), *Special issue: Social anxiety in childhood: Bridging developmental and clinical perspectives. New Directions for Child and Adolescent Development, 127,* 17–31.

Rosso, I., Olson, E., Britton, J., Stewart, S., Papadimitrious, G., Killgore, W., Makris, N., Wilhelm, S., Jenike, M., & Rauch, S. (2014). Brain white matter integrity and association with age at onset in pediatric obsessive-compulsive disorder. *Biological Mood Anxiety Disorder, 4,* 13.

Shonkoff, J., Garner, A., Siegel, B.S., Dobbins, M. I., Earls, M. F., Garner, A. S., McGuinn, L., Pascoe, J., & Wood, D. L. (2012). The lifelong effects of early childhood adversity and toxic stress. *Pediatrics, 129(1),* 232–246.

Sink, C., & Igelman, C. N. (2004). Anxiety disorders. In F. Kline & F. Silver (Eds.), *The educator's guide to mental health issues in the classroom* (pp. 171–191). Baltimore, MD: Brookes.

Spruyt, T. (2016). Comorbid depression and anxiety disorders: A key public health issue. *Journal of the Australian Traditional-Medicine Society, 22(4),* 224–227.

Swedo, S. (2002). Pediatric autoimmune neuropsychiatric disorders associated with streptococcal infections (PANDAS). *Molecular Psychiatry, 7,* 24–25.

Weber, A., Soreni, N., Stanley, J., Greco, A., Mendlowitz, S. Szatmari, P., Schachar, R., Mannasis, K., Pires, P., & Swinson, R. (2014). Proton magnetic resonance spectroscopy of prefrontal white matter in psychotropic naïve children and adolescents with obsessive-compulsive disorder. *Psychiatric Res, 222,* 67–74.

4

Signs and Symptoms of Anxiety Disorders

What if my stomach starts to hurt, what if I won't be close to
a bathroom, what if no one likes me, why can't I be normal?
Middle School Student

Mr. Hernandez is teaching seventh-grade English this
year. He looks over his class lists and arranges a meeting with
Mrs. Yasheko, who had many of these students the year before.
She voices concerns about some students in the group: At least
five had faced traumatic events during the year; a few fidgeted
a great deal; some worried, and one would cry when getting an
assignment back if it had even one correction; a few would become upset if the class routine was changed. Mr. Hernandez asks
Mrs. Yasheko if any of the students were receiving help. She said
some students saw the social worker, but she was not sure which
students they were and what type of assistance they were getting.
She had been concerned about these five students in particular
but did not know whether their symptoms were serious enough
to request that they receive more help. Mr. Hernandez now wonders what signs and symptoms he should look for and which ones

he should be concerned about. While he respects and appreciates Mrs. Yasheko's observations, he wants to form his own opinions.

Educators faced with this dilemma may wonder what warning signs and symptoms should be heeded.

Introduction to Signs and Symptoms of Anxiety Disorders

Educators play an integral part in looking for warning indicators. The presence of some may not denote a specific anxiety disorder, but they may cause the educator to reflect on whether there are patterns that are consistent over time.

Sink and Igleman (2004) used an early model of breaking down the symptoms into three areas:

1. Subjective feelings such as discomfort, worry, or fear.
2. Overt behaviors such as withdrawal or avoidance of tasks.
3. Physiological responses such as sweating, nausea, or muscle tension.

When these warning signs are ignored, or students do not get the help they need, anxiety disorders may occur and can have serious long-term effects. Anxiety disorders are a gateway to depression, substance abuse, and underachievement in school (Crawley et al., 2014; Raknes et al., 2017). If students can get early assistance, their prognosis for a healthy life is increased. The early onset and chronic nature of anxiety disorders necessitates early identification and intervention (Edwards, Rapee, Kennedy, & Spence, 2010). The symptoms of anxiety disorders tend to increase with age (Green, Berkovits, & Baker, 2015).

More recent work, since Sink and Igelman (2004), broke the signs and symptoms down into cognitive, emotional, behavioral, and physiological components. It is under these four components that we discuss these areas (Luebbe, Bell, Allwood, Swenson, & Early, 2010).

Overlap can occur in these specific areas: Behavioral inhibition can be viewed in an emotional light because of the temperamental disposition, but it can also be seen in overt behavior where the student refuses to participate in a specific activity.

Another overlap may be seen in cognitive inflexibility related to either cognition or emotion. A student, Eva, complains of tummy aches and asks to go to the restroom at least 10 times during the school day. Sometimes the teacher asks, "Do you REALLY have to go"? She wiggles with discomfort and tries to hold back tears, insisting she really does have to go. Sometimes, five minutes after returning to class, she asks again to be excused. The teacher sends her to the nurse and consults with her parents, ascertaining that the child has no medical condition that would warrant stomachaches and excessive bathroom trips.

Students like Eva may be experiencing anxiety. With or without a diagnosis, students who exhibit behaviors of anxiety deserve opportunities to achieve success in school.

Definitions of Various Warning Signs

Cognitive Signs

Problems with social information processing have been linked to anxiety disorders. Previous work, investigating the signs of anxiety disorders and depression, has focused on affective and physiological components, while research now focuses on the cognitive domain. Children with anxiety problems may interpret situations in a negative way, but they are able to recognize positive possibilities in social interactions and can respond appropriately. This is not as true for children who are depressed (Luebbe, Bell, Allwood, Swenson, & Early, 2010). These authors argue that it is important to consider both affective and social information processing when determining possible anxiety. Because of the cognitive connection, cognitive behavioral therapy has shown promise with students with anxiety disorders. When students are shown how to regulate negative and positive emotional experiences, their social information processing may improve.

While educators should never engage in therapy, the following thinking distortions, recognized by cognitive behavioral therapy, may help him recognize unusual student thinking or behavior:

Mind Reading: Assuming you know what other people think
Personalizing: Thinking you deserve the majority of blame
for something while discounting others' responsibility

Fortune Telling: Making predictions that bad things will happen without actually knowing that this is the case

All or Nothing Thinking: Thinking of people or situations in black and white terms. . . .

Catastrophizing: Believing the outcome of a situation will be so terrible that you won't be able to handle it

Labeling: Assigning a one word descriptor to the entirety of a person

Overgeneralizing: Assuming something based on a limited amount of experience

Negative Filtering/Discounting Positives: Focusing on negatives while framing positives as unimportant. . . .

(Cognitive Behavior Therapy Los Angeles, 2014)

Distorted cognitive processing is believed to be associated with the development of anxiety. While cognitive distortion can be seen in threat-related attentional bias of individuals, the evidence is not as strong for children as for adults. In one study, attentional bias did not differ between adolescents with or without anxiety disorders (Vervoort et al., 2011).

The rates of other disorders occurring along with anxiety have been found to be higher for children with intellectual disabilities than for those with attention disorders. Children with intellectual disabilities have fewer emotional regulation skills and have more difficulty expressing themselves verbally; they may be more likely to act out or engage in work refusal when they are anxious. Having a lower cognitive ability is believed to put children at a higher risk for anxiety than typical students (Green, Berkovits, & Baker, 2015).

Emotional Signs

Emotions are crucial to student success: Children and adults must be able to incorporate emotions into thinking. Emotions guide problem-solving, decision-making, and motivation to learn. In an interview with Varlas, neuroscientist Dr. Mary Helen Immordino-Yang commented that all thinking is both emotional and cognitive at the same time. It is not possible for someone to remember or think deeply about something if they have not felt emotionally about it (Varlas, 2018).

Children with anxiety and depression have reported greater experiences of negative emotions (Luebbe, Bell, Allwood, Swenson, & Early, 2010). Children with a more secure attachment history have lower levels of anxiety; children with negative emotionality or shyness showed higher levels of anxiety; children with negative emotionality during their preschool years had higher levels of anxiety as they approached preadolescence. More insecurity increased the risk of anxiety disorders (Brumariu & Kerns, 2013).

Children who exhibit fearful temperaments are at high risk for anxiety disorders. Temperament refers to the child's constitutional makeup in behavioral or emotional responsiveness. Fearful temperaments can be reflected in behavioral inhibition where the child is afraid to take chances or engage in certain activities. The emotions can be described as fearfulness, shyness, withdrawal, or inhibition (Rapee & Coplan, 2010). Many measures of anxiety focus on overt behaviors and physical symptoms, which will be discussed further, but the emotional component is an important sign or symptom for the educator to investigate.

At the preschool age, Coplan, Arbeau, and Armer (2008) found that there were associations between parent reports of shyness and teacher reports of anxiety being observed in the child.

Social anxiety disorder shares many features with shyness or withdrawal. Features of panic disorder, separation anxiety, and specific phobias are more distinct from temperament.

Behavioral Signs

There are standard behavioral symptoms that assist us in recognizing anxiety. Obvious symptoms may include becoming upset easily by mistakes, crying, frequently expressing worry, and avoiding danger. Other less obvious behavioral attributes can include irritability, anger, and failure to follow rules. Educators might confuse anxiety-based behavior with oppositional behavior.

Anxiety has an effect on attention and working memory; a student may not be consistent in her ability to perform certain academic activities because of anxiety. A teacher might think the student is not motivated when anxiety is interfering with their performance on a task.

Cognitive flexibility is the ability to shift cognitive sets and is an integral part of executive function skills. Children, by an appropriate age, need to be able to shift their focus and attention. When children do not have this ability to cognitively shift their focus, it may be related to an anxiety disorder (Affrunti & Woodruff-Borden, 2015). These children crave rigidity, routines, and sameness in the classroom. Some children, when faced with a difficult situation, are not flexible and cannot change their anxious thoughts.

Self-regulation is the ability to calm oneself down and to manage frustration. Students with anxiety may have significant difficulty with this, are unable to recognize the thought patterns that increase their anxiety, or cannot manage their thoughts (Minahan & Rappaport, 2012/2013).

Behavioral inhibition is a temperamental disposition responsible for inhibitions in response to new social and non-social events. Such inhibition, if age inappropriate, is associated with social anxiety disorder (Cunha, Soares, & Pinto-Gouveia, 2008).

Physiological Signs

Amy wiggles and wrings her hands in class constantly. With the recent incidences of flu and viruses, teachers have been emphasizing the importance of washing hands with soap and often provide hand sanitizer. For students like Amy, who is a perfectionist and struggles with anxiety, this can be counter-productive. Amy's hands are raw from excessive cleansing, yet she believes there are still germs. She asks to wash her hands every few minutes and struggles to focus on class activities. Amy's anxiety is interfering with her learning, and her fear of getting germs is taking over her life.

According to research done by Crawley et al. (2014), over 95% of youth with anxiety disorders exhibited at least one physical symptom. The number and severity of the physical symptoms is positively associated with the severity of the anxiety. Youth with generalized anxiety disorders and social anxiety disorders reported more severe and higher numbers of physical symptoms than students with social phobia. Children with comorbid anxiety and depression exhibit more physical symptoms than those with anxiety alone. Children may exhibit physical symptoms such as insomnia and fatigue. Crawley et al. (2014) stress that an evaluation for anxiety disorders is needed when students are exhibiting frequent physical complaints, such as headaches, stomachaches, insomnia, drowsiness, and sniffles.

It was suggested that when students have anxiety disorders with pervasive physical distress that the need for more evaluation determining the chronicity, impairment, and medical treatment associated with the complaints is needed. Some parents sought treatment for the physical complaints rather than for the psychological symptoms, yet these children will need an integrative treatment approach. Children with continual functional physical complaints have marked disabilities and may be involved in very invasive and expensive medical treatments (Warner et al., 2011).

Some children will focus their anxiety onto bodily functions. They might develop stomachaches, headaches, experience frequent urination, or bowel movements. These children may often ask the teacher to go to the school nurse. They make themselves sick because of the stress. The pain can go away when the child is no longer under stress (Silver, 2004).

Children may convince themselves that something is wrong with them. They may have been taken several places for evaluations, they may have heard people talking about them, and they then express their fears and worries into hypochondria. They complain that their back hurts or that they have a bad headache. These aches and pains, not to be minimized, become a child's rationalization for failure. They convince themselves and try to convince others that they cannot do something or did not do as well as they could have done because they were too sick (Silver, 2004).

What These Warning Signs Mean for Educators

When the educator begins to see worrisome signs exhibited by students that are significantly different from the behaviors of other students, the educator should first document the signs in writing. Sink and Igelman (2004) suggest documenting the following: Which signs were observed, when were they observed, and where were they observed?

The educator should frequently review these documented signs to determine whether they are getting better or worse or if there is a pattern to the behavior: Is it worse on Monday or Friday? Is it consistent all week long? Are there certain subject areas that are of particular concern? Where does the behavior occur? If the educator is able to do so, he should estimate the duration of a sign: Did the child shake or perspire when given a math assignment, and, if so, how long was the behavior seen? It is helpful if the educator can comment on the intensity of the behavior: Did both legs tremble or just one (Sink & Igelman, 2004)?

Some children will have a diagnosed anxiety disorder, others will not. Some symptoms may be mild; other symptoms will be obvious and very serious. Regardless of a diagnosis, teachers may be the only connection to possible intervention and treatment (Sink & Igelman, 2004).

It is difficult for educators to differentiate normal anxiety from a serious anxiety disorder. Understanding some of the symptoms discussed in this chapter may be helpful. Anxiety is hard to understand because it is a hidden disability, and the student may have inconsistent anxiety-related behaviors. Some students show recognizable signs; others do not (Minahan & Rappaport, 2012/2013).

TEN TEACHING TIPS

1. Document in writing the specific behaviors that you see.
2. Look for increases or decreases in those behaviors.
3. Discuss your concerns with pupil personnel, such as the social worker or school psychologist.
4. Talk to the parents, not to judge, but to determine how you can work together with them to assist their child.
5. Teach students the skills to regulate both negative and positive emotional experiences to assist students in their social information processing.
6. Engage students in goal setting and problem-solving, both of which are especially important in social situations.
7. Watch for signs of anxiety when students frequently complain of stomachaches and headaches, or are making frequent trips to the bathroom.
8. Consult with the school nurse to assist in determining whether there are physical causes for the child's discomfort.

9. Prepare students for any change in structure or routine in the classroom, while at the same time teach students how to adapt to change.
10. Watch for signs that a student cannot regulate his or her emotions, becomes upset with changes in routine, isolates herself from others, and/or complains of physical aches and pains.

Creative Connections

A Calming Collage

Sometimes students may need an activity to help them calm down when they are over anxious. A Calming Collage is a project that can be done either individually or as a group. Each collage needs two calming components: one the act of selecting and the other the act of creating, with each component calming and satisfying in and of itself.

Materials

A large envelope for each person or group labeled with their names; a variety of old magazines, such as *National Geographic*, pop culture, car, food, sports, outdoor living, home decor; poster board for the base of the collage; glue sticks or paste; and scissors.

Directions

This activity can be done as an individual project or students can work in small groups. Working in small groups allows for discussion, consensus of design, and opportunities to engage collaboratively.

The first component is to ask students to tear or cut pictures from old magazines to use to make a collage. The very act of leafing through magazines, not actually reading but looking at pictures, is calming. Ripping or cutting the pictures out is also cathartic. The act of using the images to create the collage is the second calming component of this project.

Have students choose a color they consider to be calming and ask them to select magazine pictures that they also consider calming, with shades of this color. Use prompts to guide them: Are pictures of trees, flowers, landscapes, seascapes, flowing fabric, or hair blowing in the breeze calming? Some images might pertain to specific words: black-printed words on white backgrounds or white letters printed on black or colored backgrounds; pictures of eyes; or images of nature like skies, water, trees, or animals. By ripping, tearing, or cutting, have the students select calming pictures from magazines in shades of the color chosen. Collect the various torn or cut pieces of paper in the large envelope for storage.

If the students wish to decide on a composition, it should be something that represents calm to them. Draw or have a student draw the composition on a very large piece of cardboard or poster board; mark the different areas of the picture in terms of light, dark, specific colors, or other important cues, so the students can use specific images to be incorporated into the background.

After the students have collected the magazine images, they can then begin to lay out different parts of the collage, resizing and reshaping them. If they are creating a composition, they will follow the lines and cues of the design. Some students may prefer to glue as they go, and the teacher might want to encourage them to wait so that they can organize their pictures in different ways to find the layout they like best. When the pieces are in a pleasing design that covers the entire poster board, the student may then begin to glue them in place, piece by piece.

Alternative 1

Have the students think of one object that they associate with calming. Use prompts to guide them: What objects make you feel calm? Is a musical note representative of listening to calming music? Students will then draw their image on a plain piece of construction paper and cut out the image, which is called a "silhouette." After the selected colored pieces are glued and dried, the silhouette can be glued onto the collage.

Alternative 2

Each student can write about their collage, why they chose that particular theme, why they felt the images were calming, or simply make up a story, poem, or song to go along with the collage.

Being a Change Agent

Giving students the opportunity to creatively solve a problem empowers them to have a sense of control in their lives. It is important to give students an opportunity to engage in goal setting and problem-solving in social settings. Collaborative problem-solving gives students validation and promotes the importance of creativity and seeing a variety of options for solving problems.

Directions

Step 1. Brainstorm as a group to identify issues or problems relevant to the students, such as beautifying the school environment, designing a school playground, creating a sustainable garden, reducing the school's carbon footprint, or improving public opinion of the school. List all ideas presented, without judgment, and display them for the whole group—the more creative the ideas, the better.

Step 2. Research the practicality of the various solutions with students working independently or in pairs. The students' research might include interviews, photographs, and others forms of documentation.

Step 3. Presentation of information gleaned from research by each individual or pair is made to the whole group. Decide as a group which solution is best for each issue/problem.

Step 4. Select the issue or problem the entire group wants to work on by discussing practicality and student interest.

Step 5. Create a plan of action with the students, including a timeline of events, list of materials, permissions if any must be obtained, safety plan(s), and a task list. Each task should have an assigned student(s) to oversee that task's completion.

Step 6. Implement the plan and revise, as needed, when the unexpected happens.

Step 7. Evaluate. Give the students, at the completion of the project, the opportunity to highlight successes and comment on the process. Possible prompts may include: Which parts of the collaboration were most successful? What was most problematic? What would you do differently if you could start over and do it again?

Step 8. Publicity validates the students' experiences and demonstrates the role of creativity in problem-solving. Ask the school about rules governing publicity, such as television stations, newspapers, and social media. Display the finished work, and, if appropriate, let the public know when and where it may be viewed.

Step 9. Celebrate the students' success by throwing a party, inviting parents, school faculty, and the school board.

KEY TAKEAWAYS

- Teachers play a critical role in identifying students who may or may not have anxiety disorders.

- Signs and symptoms of anxiety disorders can be exhibited through cognitive skills, emotions, overt behaviors, or physiological indicators.

- Students who may have anxiety disorders show signs of a lack of cognitive flexibility.

- Having difficulty processing social information may indicate an anxiety disorder.

- Students with possible anxiety disorders have difficulty with self-regulation.

- Students may have real physiological symptoms when they are under stress or can have imagined physical symptoms as a reason for them to explain failure.

REFERENCES

Affrunti, N., & Woodruff-Borden, J. (2015). The associations of executive function and temperament in a model of risk for childhood anxiety. *Journal of Child and Family Studies, 24,* 715–724.

Brumariu, L., & Kerns, K. (2013). Pathways to anxiety: Contributions of attachment history, temperament, peer competence, and ability to manage intense emotions. *Child Psychiatry and Human Development, 44,* 504–515.

Cognitive Behavior Therapy Los Angeles. (2014). Restructuring your thoughts by recognizing cognitive distortions. Retrieved on October 9, 2018 from cogbtherapy.com/cbtblog/2014/5/18/cognitive distortions

Coplan, R., Arbeau, K., & Armer, M. (2008). Don't fret, be supportive! Maternal characteristics linking child shyness to psychosocial and school adjustment in kindergarten. *Journal of Abnormal Child Psychology, 36,* 359–371.

Crawley, S. A., Caporino, N. E., Birmaher, B., Ginsburg, G., Piacentini, J., Albano, A. M., Sherrill, J., Sakolsky, D., Compton, S. N., Rynn, M., McCracken, J., Gosch, E., Keeton, C., March, J., Walkup, J. T., Kendall, P. C. (2014). Somatic complaints in anxious youth. *Child Psychiatry and Human Development, 45,* 398–407.

Cunha, M., Soares, I., & Pinto-Gouveia, J. (2008). The role of individual temperament, family and peers in social anxiety disorder: A controlled study. *International Journal of Clinical and Health Psychology, 8(3),* 631–655.

Edwards, S., Rapee, R., Kennedy, S., & Spence, S. (2010). The assessment of anxiety symptoms in preschool-aged children: The Revised Preschool Anxiety Scale. *Journal of Clinical Child and Adolescent Psychology, 39(3),* 400–409.

Green, S., Berkovits, L., & Baker, B. (2015). Symptoms and development of anxiety in children with and without intellectual disability. *Journal of Clinical Child and Adolescent Psychology, 44(1),* 137–144.

Luebbe, A., Bell, D., Allwood, M., Swenson, L., & Early, M. (2010). Social information processing in children: Specific relations to anxiety, depression, and affect. *Journal of Clinical Child and Adolescent Psychology, 39(3),* 386–399.

Minahan, J., & Rappaport, N. (2012/2013). Anxiety in students: A hidden culprit in behavior issues. *Kappan, 94(4),* 34–39.

Raknes, S., Pallesen, S., Himle, J., Bjaastad, J., Wergeland, G., Hoffart, A., Dyregrov, K., Haland, A., & Haugland, B. (2017). Quality of life in anxious adolescents. *Child Adolescent Psychiatry Mental Health, 11(33),* 1–11.

Rapee, R., & Coplan, R. (2010). Conceptual relations between anxiety disorder and fearful temperament. In H. Gazelle &

K. Rubin (Eds.), *Social anxiety in childhood: Bridging developmental and clinical perspectives: New directions for child and adolescent development 12* (pp. 17–31). San Francisco, CA: Jossey-Bass.

Silver, L. (2004). Brain-mind emotional interactions in the classroom. In F. Kline & L. Silver (Eds.), *The educator's guide to mental health issues in the classroom* (pp. 9–23). Baltimore, MD: Brookes.

Sink, C., & Igelman, C. (2004). Anxiety disorders. In F. Kline and L. Silver (Eds.), *The educator's guide to mental health issues in the classroom* (pp. 171–191). Baltimore, MD: Brookes.

Varlas, L. (2018). Emotions are the rudder that steers thinking. *ASCD Education Update, 60(6)*, 1, 4–5.

Vervoort, L., Wolters, L., Hogendoorn, S., Prins, P., de Haan, E., Boer, F., & Hartman, C. (2011). Temperament, attentional processes, and anxiety: Diverging links between adolescents with and without anxiety disorders. *Journal of Clinical Child and Adolescent Psychology, 40(1)*, 144–155.

Warner, C., Colognori, D., Kim, R., Reigada, L., Klein, R., Browner-Elhanan, K., Sabroksy, A., Petkova, E., Reiss, P., Chhabra, M., McFarlane-Ferreira, Y., Phoon, C., Phil, M., Pittman, N., & Benkov, K. (2011). Cognitive-behavioral treatment of persistent functional somatic complaints and pediatric anxiety: An initial controlled trial. *Depression and Anxiety, 28*, 551–559.

5

Impact of Anxiety on Social Skills

I feel worse when others get frustrated with me when my anxiety peaks. But no one is more frustrated than I am with myself for letting this happen. Again.

Student, Age 12

LIVE FROM THE CLASSROOM

Mrs. Myerson has been teaching fifth grade for over 20 years. This year she has two students who show various signs of anxiety and three with diagnosed anxiety disorders. Maria becomes upset when the classroom routine is changed or when another student gets too close to her. Another student is unable to read or answer questions when called on. The third student is preoccupied with germs and fears he will catch a bug. Mrs. Myerson has employed mindfulness techniques to accommodate their needs. She has taught her students to respect the space of all students, works to keep her routine consistent, and avoids situations that require responses out loud. Mrs. Myerson is also concerned that these children do not have friends.

Introduction to Social Skills

When a student's anxiety impacts their social skills, they can face peer rejection. Peer rejection may be associated with behavioral and emotional problems. Having friends can protect children from depression and substance abuse problems (Settipani & Kendall, 2013). Angelico, Crippa, and Loureiro (2013) argue that the excess of interpersonal anxiety, the difficulties in processing in cognitive-affective terms, the negative self-perceptions, and the self-focused attention of individuals with social anxiety disorders may result in performance or fluency deficits.

Social skills are life skills and an integral part of success in school. Individuals who have deficits in social skills lose jobs and struggle with companionship and friendship. Social skills keep people connected and provide friends who can listen and support.

Social skills is defined as the "descriptive aspect of the verbal and non-verbal behavior displayed by the individual before the different demands of interpersonal situations" (Angelico, Crippa, & Loureiro, 2013, p. 95). It is distinguished from social performance or the displaying of a behavior or sequence of behaviors in a specific social situation.

Learning is enhanced when students have the skills and competencies to manage emotions, navigate relationships, and persist in the face of adversity. Behavior and achievement may be enhanced by programs that focus on social and emotional development. Interpersonal skills include the ability to read social cues, manage social situations, resolve conflicts, work cooperatively as a team, and show compassion and empathy for other individuals (Jones & Kahn, 2017–2018). Children with anxiety disorder experience impaired social functioning.

Worry is a common denominator in all anxiety disorders. Anxiety can be about separation, worry about something catastrophic happening, or being judged in social situations. When a child is worried, it is difficult for him to concentrate on anything other than the worry. Creating a warm and nurturing environment, and having clear expectations and routines can reduce student stress. Anxiety can be an "undetected accomplice" in children's academic and social problems (Wood, 2006, p. 349).

Social Anxiety Disorder

What Can Be Learned from the Research?

SAD is the most common pediatric anxiety disorder, resulting in marked and persistent fears of social situations in which students may be evaluated negatively (Scharfstein & Beidel, 2015). They will most likely avoid social interactions because they fear rejection. They suffer from "subjective distress" (Killu & Crundwell, 2016, p. 31). Their beliefs interfere with social interactions. Students who exhibit social withdrawal by age seven will continue to struggle in this area. When they are 14, they describe themselves as having low social competence, feeling isolated and lonely (Killu & Crundwell, 2016).

Do children have actual social skills deficits or just perceive that they do? Related data is inconsistent (Angelico, Crippa, & Loureiro, 2013). Social deficits may be due to behavioral inhibition as opposed to a lack of actual social skills or withdrawing during states of high anxiety.

SADs may co-occur with other social problems, including other anxiety disorders, depression, and drug abuse (Melfsen, Walitza, & Warnke, 2006). The onset of social phobia prior to age 11 predicted no recovery in adulthood, and as a result, restriction in the quality of life follows (Davidson, 1993).

What Does This Mean in the Classroom?

Social skills consist of skill, performance, and fluency. A skill deficit is when a child does not know appropriate behaviors. Performance deficit is when a child knows appropriate behavior but does not do it consistently. When the child knows the skill, performs it consistently, but not easily, it is a fluency deficit.

The traditional approach to working with these children is often social skills training (Cartwright-Hatton, Hodges, & Porter, 2003). It should not be assumed that students have social skills problems; they may simply perceive themselves as having social skills problems. Individuals who are socially anxious underestimate their social skills (Cartwright-Hatton, Hodges, & Porter, 2003). Social anxiety can lead to limited opportunities to practice their social skills.

If students already have social skills, encourage them to perform and practice those skills. Each time the student engages in an appropriate social interaction, the behavior should be reinforced. Good behavior cannot be taken for granted; it needs to be reinforced.

Educators can model appropriate social skills. Students can learn coping skills by observing others in stressful situations.

Selective Mutism

What Can Be Learned from the Research?

Selective mutism occurs in young children and is more common in girls (Cunningham, McHolm, & Boyle, 2006). Selective mutism can range from children who only speak to family members, to those who may also speak to other adults in the community, but not to teachers or other students at school. Other children may interact verbally with peers, so the teacher does not hear what is being said. This would be a case of specific mutism. This can be considered a form of social phobia or a SAD. Up to 97% of mute children meet the criteria for social phobia or SAD. A family history of mutism has been reported in 70% of first-degree relatives (Sharkey & McNicholas, 2008).

One of the criteria of selective mutism is interference with social communication and may be prevalent in infancy or early childhood. At school, they express a fear of being judged, exhibit avoidance behaviors, and may show physical symptoms when placed in difficult social situations. A traumatic event during the early years of speech/language development has been seen in as many as one-third of children who have been studied (Andersson & Thomsen, 1988).

Annie, an eight-year-old girl, would not speak to her teacher, Mrs. Horoschak, or to anyone at school. When socks were donated to the art room, the teacher decided to have her students make sock puppets. Annie made a sock puppet, looked at the puppet, and within the teacher's hearing verbally called it "Annie." From that point forward, Annie spoke to her teacher in the classroom and in the hallway (Horoschak, 2018).

What Does This Mean in the Classroom?

While it may be difficult to understand why a student does not want to talk, the teacher needs to be patient. There may be a variety of reasons the child does not talk. To force them to engage in an interaction will not work and can make the situation worse. Strive to establish a warm and nurturing environment where positive interaction with a peer or another adult is reinforced.

Generalized Anxiety Disorder

What Can Be Learned from the Research?

Generalized anxiety disorder (GAD) is characterized by excessive worry. Students may establish high and often unrealistic expectations for their performance. They are eager to please and often seek continual reassurance. They are overly conscientious and may be perfectionists (Scharfstein & Beidel, 2015).

Children who are anxious may suffer from peer neglect and rejection (Scharfstein, Alfano, Beidel, & Wong, 2011). They may be reticent, avoid peer interaction, and can act in a less competent manner because they perceive a threat (Wood, 2006).

Scharfstein and Beidel (2015) found that children with both SAD and GAD have greater difficulties in interpersonal relationships than those without anxiety. Children with SAD feel invalidated within their closest friendships and therefore lack trust. Children with GAD reported impaired interpersonal relationships, yet their peers positively rated them on reliability and friendship potential.

What Does This Mean in the Classroom?

Children with GAD need continual reassurance through modeling and positive reinforcement of social performance skills. Avoid stress-provoking situations, like requiring students to read or speak in front of their peers. This requires teachers know their students and their stress-provoking triggers.

Panic Disorder

What Can Be Learned from the Research?

Panic attacks may occur as a result of a traumatic experience. Bilodeau, Bradwejn, and Koszycki (2015) found that the ability to read facial emotions was important for adaptive social skills, emotional development, and well-being. This ability develops further as children get older. The inability to process facial emotion has been observed in children with a wide range of psychological problems, which include anxiety disorders. Children who are anxious make mistakes in recognizing negative faces or mislabel positive or neutral emotions. Data suggests educators work on teaching children to discriminate between negative versus positive feelings.

Children and adolescents can have symptoms similar to adult panic attacks. Panic attacks in children can result in an increased heart rate, tingling and numbing situations, hot or cold flushes, inability to move, or even terror. The child feels intense fear and impending doom.

What Does This Mean in the Classroom?

Panic attacks can be accompanied by agoraphobia, which is the fear of being stuck in a situation where there is no help or escape available. Educators need to provide assurance that they are there to help these students.

Picture this true story of Ryan, a teenager, who had a panic disorder related to heights. On a class field trip, Ryan panicked and started gasping for air near the elevator. He could not move. The teacher sent the rest of the class with chaperones up the elevator and took Ryan to climb the stairs. This teenager gripped his teacher's hand as they took three steps and then paused. Ryan was dripping sweat, and his hands were clammy. The teacher praised and encouraged him. They made it up one flight of stairs, and the teacher determined that it was too difficult for Ryan to go the rest of the way. The teacher directed the chaperones to continue and meet them later at the bottom of the stairs.

None of the other students were aware of what had happened, and Ryan and the teacher were glad the experience was over. The teacher knew that it was important not to embarrass any student in front of his peers.

Students who have difficulty reading facial expressions can be taught what specific facial cues mean. Teachers can show students pictures and discuss the expressions.

Separation Anxiety Disorder

What Can Be Learned from the Research?

Separation Anxiety Disorder is defined as an abnormal reaction to real or imagined separation from attachment figures; interfering with daily activities, the ability to concentrate, and social relationships with others. It is prevalent in 4%–5% of all children and 50%–75% of children who come from homes of low socioeconomic status. The mean age of onset is seven and a half years (Masi, Mucci, & Millepiedi, 2001).

Separation Anxiety Disorder may be a risk factor for other types of anxiety disorders. It is a specific risk factor for adult panic disorder and a general risk factor for multiple adult anxiety disorders (Kossowsky, Wilhelm, Roth, & Schneider, 2012; Kossowsky et al., 2013). A childhood diagnosis of separation anxiety significantly increases the likelihood of panic disorder in adulthood and the risk of other anxiety disorders (Kossowsky et al., 2013).

What Does This Mean in the Classroom?

Students with separation anxiety need patience and understanding. During school drop-off, a crying child may be comforted by holding the teacher's hand or becoming the teacher's assistant. Other students may need a more involved intervention. Russell had good attendance at school until his father died while Russell was at school. His mother had a number of health concerns, which caused Russell to fear that his mother would die while he was away from her. Russell became socially isolated from everyone except his mother and refused to attend school. His mother and school professionals planned an intervention that included her volunteering at school until he felt comfortable.

Obsessive-Compulsive Disorder

What Can Be Learned from the Research?

The *Diagnostic and Statistical Manual of Mental Disorders, Fifth Edition* (DSM-5; American Psychiatric Association, 2013) removed OCD and PTSD from under the heading of anxiety disorders, and they are now stand-alone disorders (Moller & Bogels, 2016). Due to the prevalence of anxiety exhibited by children with OCD and PTSD, information is included here.

Thirty-four percent of adults with OCD had it as a child (Bennett, Coughtrey, Shafran, & Heyman, 2017). If left untreated, it causes significant distress and social problems. Childhood obsessions may include unwanted thoughts, urges, and compulsions, such as repetitive and time-consuming behaviors.

OCD is sometimes hard to identify because some repetitive and ritualistic behavior is normal in young children. The telling sign for OCD is when the behaviors become distressing. Differential diagnosis is also difficult because in some children with autism, it can be hard to determine whether compulsions are driven by anxiety and distress or if a repetitive behavior is motivated by pleasure (Bennett, Coughtrey, Shafran, & Heyman, 2017).

There is a high comorbidity between OCD and anxiety. There is heterogeneity in children with pediatric OCD that appears to be related to fear (Rozenman et al., 2017).

Tourette Syndrome is often comorbid with anxiety disorders. Depending on the nature of the student's tic, the student may be isolated from peers when peers do not understand the tics. A recent study of over 1,300 children and adults with Tourette Syndrome found that the lifetime prevalence rate of individuals with Tourette Syndrome and anxiety disorders was 36.1%: 21% had GAD, 10% had OCD, and 2% had Separation Anxiety Disorder. As a result of their study, Marwitz and Pringsheim (2018) encourage early screening for anxiety in children with Tourette Syndrome.

What Does This Mean in the Classroom?

Identifying triggers of children experiencing OCD and other forms of anxiety is the first step in determining accommodations. Desmond, a nine-year-old who exhibited OCD tendencies, became upset when his math paper touched his other papers; if his papers were returned in a stack, he would throw a tantrum that could last two hours. Other children were fearful of him. Once it was determined what was triggering these tantrums, the teacher found a cardboard container with individual compartments so that Desmond could put his reading papers in one compartment, math in another, science in another, and so on.

Students with OCD and anxiety may need more time to complete tasks. If students are worried about completing the assignment perfectly, the teacher can encourage the student to submit a draft for feedback prior to the deadline.

Post-Traumatic Stress Disorder

What Can Be Learned from the Research?

Trauma in children's lives has a significant influence on cognitive structuring and coping skills. Children exposed to trauma spend a tremendous amount of energy dealing with the trauma, which can lead to weaknesses in dealing with other stressors in their lives (Olmez, Ataogulu, Kocagoz, & Pasin, 2018). While PTSD is listed in the DSM-5 separately from anxiety, many teachers have seen the high degree of anxiety as a result of PTSD. In a sample of adolescents from China who were trauma exposed, it was found that PTSD is very complex and heterogeneous (Liu, Wang, Cao, Qing, & Armour, 2016).

What Does This Mean in the Classroom?

Because of this complexity, educators should be cognizant that the traumatic events experienced by students may trigger anxiety in the classroom. Jeremy experienced flooding which destroyed the family's home. Now he has a panic attack anytime it rains, anticipating more flooding. Knowing the context of the child's anxiety can help teachers provide appropriate strategies to comfort the child.

Children may come into the classroom emotionally drained, unable to build relationships with the teacher and other students. Providing a caring and compassionate classroom with structure and routine shows children that they are safe in the environment.

The Impact of Bullying on Children with Social Anxiety

What Can Be Learned from the Research?

Bullying is a serious social problem in today's society and can trigger anxiety. More attention is being drawn to the long-term effects of bullying on students. Peer victimization is linked to emotional distress and loneliness (Lee, Shellman, Osmer, Day, & Dempsey, 2016). Social anxiety is an indicator of victimization (Pabian & Vandebosch, 2016). Being a victim of bullying has been found to be associated with several social anxiety symptoms, such as the cognitive fear of self- evaluation, loneliness, avoidance of social situations, and poor interpersonal skills (Dempsey & Storch, 2008).

When victims help other victims, this allows them to ally themselves with other victims. Students who were taught to defend victims did not experience social anxiety that children who were depressed did (Wu, Luu, & Luh, 2016). Victimization as a child may result in social anxiety as an adult (Boulton, 2013). Some of this anxiety can be moderated by positive coping and problem-solving skills but can continue to occur when individuals engage in self-blame.

Attentional bias is a term that refers to the phenomenon of hyper-attention to threatening material. The clinical consequence of attentional bias appears to increase focus on danger and threat stimuli which can perpetuate phobic fear. Attentional bias implicates an increased encoding of threatening material, and this in turn elevates fear levels (Muris & Merckelbach, 1998). This bias for threat is associated with a range of anxiety disorders (Mogg, Wilson, Hayward, Cunning, & Bradley, 2012).

What Does This Mean in the Classroom?

Appropriate coping skills can result in positive social skills. Emotional or avoidance coping can result in additional peer victimization. Teachers must be diligent in reducing peer victimization, so students feel safe as well as teaching positive and adaptive coping skills to reduce the social anxiety that students may experience in school. Students working collaboratively may reduce bullying.

FIVE TEACHING TIPS

1. Strive to understand the context of students' anxiety by active listening and by talking with parents, students, and previous teachers.

2. Teach students how to read specific facial expressions.
3. Teach positive and adaptive coping skills.
4. Create a bully-free classroom environment by teaching the students kindness and acceptance in the classroom.
5. Provide structure and routine combined with compassion and care.

Creative Connections

Painted Rocks

Painted rocks have been around for centuries but have recently regained popularity. This art project addresses social anxiety by providing students a safe, enjoyable creative activity that encourages collaboration while contributing to the well-being of others. Students can work independently painting colorful rocks with words and images representing strength and joy. Emphasize that just as no two rocks are the same, no two people are the same.

Materials

Rocks of various sizes and shapes, acrylic paint in assorted colors, small paintbrushes, plastic containers for water, paper towels, and clear acrylic spray sealer.

Directions

Students choose a rock and paint using acrylic paint. After the paint is dry, each student then places his or her rock on a piece of paper and writes their name on that paper next to their rock. The teacher seals all rocks with a clear acrylic spray sealant (spray outside or in well-ventilated area). After the rocks are dry, have students sit in a circle and ask them to share their artistic decisions.

Encourage reflections by asking, *Why did you choose those colors and images? What do you do to be strong? What brings you joy and strength?* Then each student who has spoken, or "passed," hands their rock to the person on their right. By the time every student has shared or "passed," each person should have their own artistic rock back. Their rock touched by all students in the class can be a reminder of many sources of strength shared by every person in class.

Students can put their rock on a window sill or on their desk. Encourage them, the next time they feel anxious, to hold this rock in their hand. Remind them that everyone has challenges and different sources of strength and joy. The rock can be a reminder of a student's own strengths, or they can borrow an idea of strength and joy that was heard from a classmate.

> **Alternative #1:** Instead of having students keep their own rock, have students create community art by hiding the rocks somewhere in the community in a public place for others to find.
>
> **Alternative #2:** Have students create a community sculpture in the school or neighborhood by arranging the colorful rocks somewhere in the landscape. Remember to get permission first.
>
> **Alternative #3:** Have students paint kindness rocks with up-lifting messages on them intended for others, and place in community settings to spread happiness. Messages can include: *Have a nice day! Smile! Kindness Rocks!*

Puppets

Perhaps the most famous puppets in the world are the Muppets on *Sesame Street*. Puppetry is an ancient art form, believed to have developed over the last 3,000 years. Messages about childhood concepts, such as sharing, playing fair, or recognizing bullying, are often presented through puppetry. Puppets can be used as a safe way for traumatized children to explore their fears (*History of Puppetry*, 2018). According to *Puppets: Art and Amusement*, by Suzanne Pemsler and The Puppet Divas (2018): "[P]uppets communicate with or without words. They confront human fears and conflicts, improvise, problem solve, and move audiences to new worlds. They seem to listen to one another, feel emotion, and think" (Pemsler and the Puppet Divas, 2018).

Children of all ages can create their own puppets to present their own story, a favorite story, or to be part of a group production. Having a theme for the puppets, such as superheroes, animals, machines, or characters from a favorite story, inspires students. The puppets can be individuals, or part of a group, such as the child or monsters in Maurice Sendak's *Where the Wild Things Are* (1963).

Pre-K to Eighth-Grade Sock Puppets

Materials

Providing a large variety of materials will enhance the creative experience for children. Consider a variety of felt, scraps of yarn, lace, plastic googly eyes, beads, ribbons, and any other fun embellishments you might have; fabric or tacky glue, markers, scissors (do not forget the lefties!), and tube socks for the puppets (socks of different colors is fun and adds to the personality of each puppet); and popsicle sticks for applying glue. Older children (tweens and older) can use a low-temperature hot glue gun. Egg cartons and Styrofoam trays help keep materials organized. A layer of newspaper or a plastic tablecloth will help with cleanup. Although sock puppets are usually for younger children, high school students have successfully enjoyed this project, adding more sophisticated materials, such as silks, velvets, faux rhinestone gems, feathers, discarded jewelry, leather, and other more age-appropriate materials.

Directions

Have all materials organized for children to use. For young children, have a variety of colorful precut felt pieces in assorted shapes, such as circles, ovals, triangles, and shapes one might associate with human or animal characters. Older children sometimes need a few prompts to get their ideas going. Remind the children that they can decorate the bodies of their puppets too.

Always start with a teacher demonstration of each step. Have the children create a mouth shape, tongue, or teeth before starting, as that is the first step in decorating the sock puppet. Place your hand into the sock, and decide where the mouth will be. This is done by folding your thumb to your other four fingers and pretending to make your sock puppet talk. Mark this area and glue on a tongue, teeth, or mouth of some sort. Continue decorating until your sock puppet is finished. Encourage the children to have fun designing the puppet experimenting with ideas for clothing or puppet bodies. Be sure to allow the glue to dry.

Middle and High School Students Puppetry

Older students and young adults enjoy making sock puppets, providing outlets for communication using the art of play. However, in addition to the more sophisticated materials listed above, you can use more advanced art media and processes for older students; substitute paper mâché or plaster craft puppets instead of sock puppetry.

Materials

For paper mâché, you will need a lot of newspaper and some type of adhesive, such as paper mâché glue. There are commercial products available for purchase, but a mixture of equal parts flour and water mixed to a thin consistency will work. Plaster craft material is similar to the plaster used for making medical casts so hardens without an adhesive. When working with either media, you will also need the following: balloons for puppet heads (various sizes and shapes), poster board, masking tape, individual plastic water containers, scissors, paper towels, paint, more newspapers, a strong craft glue to attach the heads to the bodies, low-temperature hot glue guns, scrap fabrics, beads, feathers, trinkets, faux gems, yarn scraps, and any other fun materials with which to decorate the puppets.

Workspace Preparation

This tends to be a messy project, so prepare by covering the work area with layers of newspaper or plastic cloths. Have a "disposal bucket" available so that the students can dump their dirty water into the bucket and not down the drain, which might cause a drain problem. (The water can later be disposed of in the building mop room).

The projects will have to dry, so set aside an area for drying covered with a lot of newspaper on which to set the puppets. (Be sure the students have their names on the puppets!)

Precut strips of paper for paper mâché or plaster craft material before the students arrive. Create a designated "clean area" and "messy area." Later, decorate the puppets in a "painting area" and a "gluing area" to keep materials organized and prevent accidents. Once the puppets are completed and dried, the students will give the puppets distinct personalities through their choice of decorations. Your students may become very engrossed and lose track of time, so set a timer to alert them that cleanup time is near.

Directions

Have each student inflate a balloon, securely tying the end into a knot for the head. Caution them not to over-inflate their balloons, as the weight of the wet material will cause the balloon to pop and the puppet's head to collapse.

To form the neck of the puppet, cut a cardboard about two to four inches in height and of a length so that the circle it creates leaves enough space to insert three fingers to work the head. Tape the ring into a circle and cut small slits/tabs around the top of the ring and fold the tabs outward. Using masking tape, attach the ring to the bottom of an inflated balloon. Apply the wet material being used to the balloon and both the inside and outside of the cardboard ring (without covering the middle space for the three fingers). Cover the balloon and cardboard neck ring with a complete all-over coat before adding a second layer. Allowing the puppet to dry before adding a third coat will help strengthen the structure of the puppet head.

Special features can be built on, such as faces, ears, wrinkles, scars, and whatever the students' imaginations dictate, using the wet materials. If students don't wish to add special features, their dry puppets can be painted immediately. All painting should be dry before applying any other decorative materials, including the puppet body.

To make the puppet body, trace the student's hand with thumb out, three fingers close together, and pinkie out. The thumb and pinkie will become the arms of the puppet. Draw another line about an inch or two outside the hand drawing, all the way around, including the wrist/arm, creating something similar to a mitten or glove. This outer line will be the cutting line which will allow enough space for the student to sew or hot glue the side seams together and still allow the student's hand to fit inside the puppet's body and head. The students will then cut out the pattern and tape or pin it to the desired fabric. Two pieces of fabric will need to be cut: a front and back, which can be the same or different fabric, depending on the character of the puppet. After gluing or stitching the body together, the body can be hot glued or glued with a strong craft glue to the neck of the puppet.

The puppet is now ready for the "extras" that will define the puppet's character. Let the decorating begin: gluing hair, clothing details, jewelry, or whatever the puppet requires!

Once the puppets are completed, have each puppet give its name and tell a little about himself or herself to the other puppets and students. Encourage the students to use the voice of their puppet. Allow the puppets time to talk with each other and to have fun with their "people."

Encourage the students to create puppet shows for each other or even for other audiences.

KEY TAKEAWAYS

- Worry is the common thread in all types of anxiety disorders.

- There is an increasing number of students with anxiety disorders, which impacts their relationships with teachers and fellow students.

- Students should be positively reinforced for handling difficult situations in an appropriate manner.

- Students with anxiety disorders may have adequate social skills but perceive that they do not.

- Bias for threat is associated with a range of anxiety disorders.

REFERENCES

American Psychiatric Association (Eds.). (2013). *Diagnostic and statistical manual of mental disorders: DSM-5*. Washington, DC: American Psychiatric Association.

Andersson, C., & Thomsen, P. (1988). Electively mute children: An analysis of Danish cases. *Nordic Journal of Psychiatry, 52,* 231–238.

Angelico, A., Crippa, J., & Loureiro, S. (2013). Social anxiety disorder and social skills: A critical review of the literature. *International Journal of Behavioral Consultation and Therapy, 6(2),* 95–110.

Bennett, S., Coughtrey, A., Shafran, R., & Heyman, I. (2017). Measurement issues: The measurement of obsessive compulsive disorder in children and young people in clinical practice. *Child and Adolescent Mental Health, 22(2),* 100–112.

Bilodeau, C. Bradwejn, J., & Koszycki, D. (2015). Impaired facial affect perception in unaffected children at familial risk for Panic Disorder. *Child Psychiatry Human Development, 46,* 715–724.

Boulton, M. (2013). Associations between adults' recalled childhood bullying victimization, current social anxiety, coping, and self-blame: Evidence for moderation and indirect effects. *Anxiety, Stress, and Coping, 26(3),* 270–292.

Cartwright-Hatton, S., Hodges, L., & Porter, J. (2003). Social anxiety in childhood: The relationship with self and observer rated social skills. *Journal of Child Psychology and Psychiatry, 44(5),* 737–742.

Cunningham, C., McHolm, A., & Boyle, M. (2006). Social phobia, anxiety, oppositional behavior, social skills, and self-concept in children with specific selective mutism, generalized selective mutism, and community controls. *European Child and Adolescent Psychiatry, 15(5),* 245–255.

Davidson, J. (1993). *Childhood histories of adult social phobics.* Presented at the Anxiety Disorders Association of America Annual Convention, Charleston, SC.

Dempsey, A., & Storch, E. (2008). Relational victimization. The association between recalled adolescent social experiences and emotional adjustment in early adulthood. *Psychology in the Schools, 45,* 310–322.

History of puppetry. (2018). Retrieved on June 7, 2018 from www.theatersatstore.com/history-of-puppetry.

Horoschak, L. (2018). The deep joy of teaching art to students who have experienced trauma. In A. Hunter, D. Heise, & B. Johns, (Eds.), *Art for children experiencing psychological trauma: A guide for art educators and school-based professionals* (pp. 271–286). New York, NY: Routledge.

Jones, S., & Kahn, J. (2017–2018). The evidence base for how learning happens. *American Educator, 41(4)*, 16–21.

Killu, K., & Crundwell, R. (2016). Students with anxiety in the classroom: Educational accommodations and interventions. *Beyond Behavior, 25(2)*, 30–40.

Kossowsky, J., Wilhelm, F., Roth, W., & Schneider, S. (2012). Separation anxiety disorder in children: disorder-specific responses to experimental separation from the mother. *The Journal of Child Psychology and Psychiatry, 53(2)*, 178–187.

Kossowsky, J., Pfaltz, M., Schneider, S., Taeymans, J., Locher, C., & Gaab, J. (2013). The separation anxiety hypothesis of panic disorder revisited: A meta-analysis. *American Journal of Psychiatry, 170(7)*, 768–781.

Lee, K., Shellman, A., Osmer, S., Day, S., & Dempsey, A. (2016). Peer victimization and social anxiety: An exploration of coping strategies as mediators. *Journal of School Violence, 15*, 406–423.

Liu, L., Wang, L., Cao, C., Qing, Y., & Armour, C. (2016). Testing the dimensional structure of *DSM-5* posttraumatic stress disorder symptoms in a nonclinical trauma-exposed adolescent sample. *Journal of Child Psychology and Psychiatry, 57(2)*, 204–212.

Marwitz, L., & Pringsheim, T. (2018). Clinical utility of screening for anxiety and depression in children with Tourette syndrome. *Journal of the Canadian Academy of Child and Adolescent Psychiatry, 27(1)*, 15–21.

Masi, G., Mucci, M., & Millepiedi, S. (2001). Separation anxiety in children and adolescents. *CNS Drugs, 15(2)*, 93–104.

Melfsen, S., Walitza, S., & Warnke, A. (2006). The extent of social anxiety in combination with mental disorders. *European Child and Adolescent Psychiatry, 15(2)*, 111–117.

Mogg, K., Wilson, K., Hayward, C., Cunning, D., & Bradley, B. (2012). Attentional biases for threat in at-risk daughters and mothers with lifetime Panic Disorder. *Journal of Abnormal Psychology, 121(4)*, 852–862.

Moller, E., & Bogels, S. (2016). The DSM-5 dimensional anxiety scales in a Dutch non-clinical sample: Psychometric properties including the adult separation anxiety disorder scale. *International Journal of Methods in Psychiatric Research, 25(3)*, 232–239.

Muris, P., & Merckelbach, H. (1998). Adults: Clinical formulation and treatment. In A. Bellack & M. Hersen (Eds.), *Comprehensive clinical psychology* (Vol. 6.20, pp. 461–474). New York: Elsevier Science.

Olmez, S., Ataogulu, B., Kocagoz, Z., & Pasin, O. (2018). An investigation of childhood trauma in patients with panic disorder. *Nobel Medicus, 40,* 39–48.

Pabian, S., & Vandebosch, H. (2016). An investigation of short term longitudinal associations between social anxiety and victimization and perpetration of traditional bullying and cyberbullying. *Journal of Youth Adolescence, 45,* 328–339.

Pemsler, S., & The Puppet Divas. (2018). *Puppets: Art and amusement.* Retrieved on June 12, 2018 from www.puppets bostonguild.org/puppetry.html

Rozenman, M., Peris, T., Bergman, R., Chang, S., O'Neill, J., McCracken, J., & Piacentini, J. (2017). Distinguishing fear versus distress symptomatology in pediatric OCD. *Child Psychiatry Human Development, 48,* 63–72.

Scharfstein, L., Alfano, C., Beidel, D., & Wong, N. (2011). Children with generalized anxiety disorder do not have peer problems, just fewer friends. *Child Psychiatry Human Development* 42(6), 712–723.

Scharfstein, L., & Beidel, D. (2015). Social skills and social acceptance in children with anxiety disorders. *Journal of Clinical Child and Adolescent Psychology, 44(5),* 826–838.

Sendak, M. (1963). *Where the wild things are.* New York, NY: Harper & Row.

Settipani, C., & Kendall, P. (2013). Social functioning in youth with anxiety disorders: Association with anxiety severity and outcomes from cognitive-behavioral therapy. *Child Psychiatry Human Development, 44,* 1–18.

Sharkey, L., & McNicholas, F. (2008). More than 100 years of silence, elective mutism: A review of the literature. *European Child and Adolescent Psychiatry, 17(5),* 255–263.

Wood, J. (2006). Effect of anxiety reduction on children's school performance and social adjustment. *Developmental Psychology, 42(2),* 345–349.

Wu, W., Luu, S., & Luh, D. (2016). Defending behaviors, bullying roles, and their associations with mental health in junior high school students: A population-based study. *BMC Public Health, 16(1066),* 1–10.

6

Impact of Anxiety on Academic Skills

I wish my teachers knew that we can't help it. We try. Punishing us doesn't help. Yelling or getting frustrated with us makes it so much worse.

Student, Age 13

LIVE FROM THE CLASSROOM

Mr. Wong has been teaching high school English for 10 years. This year he is eager to see how well one of his students, Danielle, can write. Danielle's mother is a journalist, so Mr. Wong is hoping that Danielle will enjoy writing. However, he is noticing that when he gives the students a creative writing project, Danielle appears to be very nervous, starts twirling her hair, and perspiring. She says she doesn't want to write in class and asks if she can take the work home. Mr. Wong, trying to be understanding, tells her she may start the projects in class and then take them home to finish. Danielle finds all kinds of excuses why she cannot write in class and, on several occasions, asks to see the school nurse because she says she is ill.

A few weeks later, Mr. Wong conferences with Danielle's mother. Her mother reveals that she too has been very concerned about Danielle's behavior and took her to a psychologist to see if there was a problem. The clinical psychologist diagnosed Danielle with generalized anxiety disorder and began cognitive behavioral therapy. Danielle's mother hopes that there will be improvements. Even though her mother tries not to put pressure on her, Danielle believes she is always being evaluated based on her mother's writing skills.

Introduction to Anxiety Disorders

Anxiety disorders are sometimes associated with poor academic performance, school refusal, and higher school dropout rates. Students with some types of academic anxiety have a biological predisposition to high levels of anxiety when they believe that they are being evaluated (Huberty, 2009; Killu & Crundwell, 2016). Untreated childhood anxiety increases the risk in young adulthood of other problems including educational underachievement (Skryabina, Taylor, & Stallard, 2016).

Anxiety impacts academic performance as seen in an adverse effect on concentration, memory, attention, organization of work, and performance on tests and evaluative tasks (Killu & Crundwell, 2016). As seen above, Danielle believed that she was continually being evaluated on her writing because of her own mother's career. Student's perceptions can increase anxiety and have negative effects on academic performance. Therefore, when students are being evaluated for underachievement, especially as related to in-class performance, it is important to assess whether they are struggling with anxiety-related academic problems (Nail et al., 2015).

Generalized Anxiety Disorder

What Can Be Learned from the Research?

Youth with generalized anxiety disorder (GAD) have shown the highest number of specific academic impairments (Nail et al., 2015). This relates to the pervasive nature of dread and worry that can be exhibited by these students. They may have difficulty with reading aloud, giving oral reports, or giving speeches. Excessive anxiety can contribute to reduced overall functioning within the classroom, which then negatively impacts academic performance. Academic problems, such as poor grades, can increase anxiety and reduce functioning overall.

Some researchers have pinpointed specific math anxiety in students (Carey, Devine, Hill, & Szucs, 2017; Cargnelutti, Tomasetto, & Passolunghi, 2017). A study in England found changes in anxiety-specific issues between students in fourth grade and those in seventh and eighth grades. The older students with high levels of anxiety did not experience as much math anxiety as those with specifically elevated academic anxieties in general. Researchers recommend that teachers look at the student as a whole rather than focusing specifically on the math anxiety.

A low self-concept about school can be linked to test anxiety and to a poor math self-concept, which is then linked to math anxiety (Carey, Devine, Hill, & Szucs, 2017). Anxiety is present in preschool children. In Italy, math-specific test anxiety and math performance were studied in children in second and third grades. These researchers believe that math anxiety is a specified subtype of anxiety that can be experienced in the absence of both general and test anxiety. High levels of math anxiety have resulted in low performance in math. In this research, generalized anxiety disorders affected proficiency in both grades, while a significant direct role of math anxiety emerged only in third grade. The early onset of negative experiences in math is predictive of poorer proficiency over time (Cargnelutti, Tomasetto, & Passolunghi, 2017).

What Does This Mean in the Classroom?

For students with generalized anxiety disorder, teachers can eliminate any situation where all students are required to give oral reports or speeches and/or look for other ways for students to demonstrate learning. Perhaps a student may not want to present in class but is willing to record himself making a presentation and then present the tape to the class.

In mathematics, it is important not only to detect and remediate deficiencies in cognitive math skills but also to address the negative affective conditions of anxiety (Cargnelutti, Tomasetto, & Passolunghi, 2017). It is beneficial to immerse students from a young age in positive experiences with math.

Social Anxiety Disorder (SAD)

What Can Be Learned from the Research?

It has been reported by some that not all youth with social anxiety disorder (SAD) have significant academic impairments. Students may have difficulty getting to school or staying in school (Nail et al., 2015). Some teachers suggest that while these students may have ability to do well academically, they may not be performing at grade level because their anxiety interferes with their achievement. Other students seem to do well academically and are performing at grade level, but their anxiety keeps them from reaching their full potential. Some gifted students experience this.

Approximately 3%–8% of students in the United States experienced SAD (Scharfstein & Beidel, 2015). A 2016 study done with a sample of over 331 students in India, ages 13–17 years old, found a prevalence rate of 5.3% of adolescents with SAD. These students represented upper-middle class families and spoke English. Scharfstein and Beidel (2015) reported more females than males had SAD. Students with SAD performed significantly worse academically than those without SAD and found that SAD is associated with high school dropout rates (Soohinda & Sampath, 2016).

What Does This Mean in the Classroom?

Students with SAD may have the ability to do well but cannot perform because of social anxieties. Educators can look for alternative ways for students to show that they know concepts other than performing in front of a crowd, by extensive written work, or a test. The teacher should capitalize on the strengths of the student and build those strengths into the work expected. Students can be given options for demonstrating learning. For example, a student could do an artistic depiction of what they learned. Other ways include creating and presenting a poem, short story, rap, song, play, or even a dance movement. Presentations may take the form of electronic slide presentations or digital video, or may be performed for the teacher alone.

Obsessive-Compulsive Disorder (OCD)

What Can Be Learned from the Research?

Obsessions are recurring and unwanted intrusive thoughts or ideas; compulsions are the need to engage in repetitive physical or mental acts (Shafran, 2001). Children may be obsessed with failing an assignment or worried that they cannot do an assignment perfectly. A student may be worried that they have to answer every question in the exact order of which it was presented. Some cannot skim an assignment and complete the answers they know and go back to those they must ponder. They must start with #1 and finish with #20. Their obsessions and compulsions result in constant worry and constant thinking about the issue or task.

Some children with obsessive-compulsive disorder (OCD) do not exhibit the motivation to change, which may be due to a variety of reasons. They may believe that terrible disasters will happen if they do not follow the ritual; they may not believe that any interventions will work; they may exhibit a lack of self-confidence; or they may have concurrent conditions, such as depression, that interfere with their motivation to change. They may have attention-deficit hyperactivity disorder and may not be goal-directed. Or they may have oppositional defiant behavior or a conduct disorder and are resistant to change (Weidle & Skarphedinsson, 2016). Some children with OCD have been found also to have bipolar disorders. Rates of comorbidity have been reported in the range of 15%–44% of the pediatric population (Gagan et al., 2010).

Most adults with OCD exhibited symptoms before the age of 18, with an average age of onset from 7½ to 12½ years (Shafran, 2001). Boys have a higher incidence rate of OCD than girls in childhood and adolescence (Tochkov, 2011). These children's lives are consumed with fear and anxiety.

What Does This Mean in the Classroom?

To make necessary accommodations, teachers need to first be cognizant of any rituals that a student engages in before beginning or completing an academic assignment. Some children will try to hide their obsessions and compulsions. The teacher may not be aware that a student is reciting to himself a pattern of numbers, behaviors, or other compulsions before they can complete an assignment. Another student may need to read the directions to himself five times before he can begin the task. The teacher may know that the student is upset but not realize the trigger for the distress. For example, a stray mark on a worksheet might deter a student from even beginning a worksheet. If these rituals are such that the student is able to do his or her work, they will not be disruptive. If, however, they are interfering with academic work, it may cause embarrassment, which, in turn, can contribute to their anxiety. A student may need additional time to do an assignment, or the teacher may provide another worksheet if the student's copy has gotten dirty.

Some obsessions and compulsions are obvious: a student who cannot step on a crack on the floor; a student who becomes very upset at making a mistake and refuses to erase or continue; a student who begins to cry or tears the paper up and throws it on the floor because it is no longer perfect; or the student engaged in a writing assignment who has difficulty getting everything right and so keeps going over the same sentence repeatedly and cannot move on.

Taking any action that embarrasses the student in front of peers will upset the student more. Accommodations can be made according to the nature of the behavior. The teacher may want to break the writing assignment down into small steps and let the student know that he or she will proofread the work and provide feedback to the student. Positive recognition for everything the student does well is helpful as is a classroom environment that is safe and secure for the student. Private conversations with the student about how best to help are necessary and productive. The teacher will need to document all behaviors and be in ongoing communication with the social worker, psychologist, and parents to design effective accommodations.

Test Anxiety Disorder

What Can Be Learned from the Research?

Studies have shown that test anxiety decreases academic performance. Test anxiety has been documented in children as young as seven (Connor, 2003), with test anxiety estimated in

10%–40% (Putwain, 2007). Worry about failure and comparing self-performance to others are common behaviors in test anxious individuals in evaluation situations.

Worry is the most powerful component of test anxiety in academic performance (Eum & Rice, 2011; Sarason, 1988). Some worry about the consequences of failure and may engage in derogatory internal self-dialogue which disrupts cognitive functions. Individuals with maladaptive perfectionism have high performance expectations and engage in extreme self-blame when they do not live up to their expectations. Individuals with adaptive perfectionism have high performance expectations but have low levels of negative self-evaluation (Rice & Ashby, 2007). Students with test anxiety perform poorly on recall tasks and perform less well in terms of overall academic achievement (Eum & Rice, 2011).

Increased attention and emphasis on the importance of high-stakes testing often results in increased levels of test anxiety (Putwain, 2007; Von Der Embse & Hasson, 2012). This test anxiety is related to worry about the evaluative outcome of the test. Von Der Embse and Hasson (2012) found that there was no significant difference in test anxiety levels between urban schools and suburban schools.

What Does This Mean in the Classroom?

Finding ways to reduce test anxiety is beneficial for all students and is critical to those students with test anxiety disorders. The following strategies have proven successful in many classrooms. Guided relaxation immediately prior to the testing, such as deep breathing, concentrating on the positive, and giving reinforcing statements, can calm a student. Focus on positive outcomes rather than punitive ones. Students can be taught stress reducing strategies during the test, such as silent positive self-talk (Von Der Embse & Hasson, 2012). Teaching students mindfulness practices result in students being more able to control anger, negative emotions, and irrational thoughts. Such practices can also increase a student's ability to focus attention and ignore distractions, and some results have shown an increase in academic performance (Anila & Dhanalakshmi, 2016).

TEN TEACHING TIPS

1. Learn as much as you can about the student's type of anxiety and the obsessions/compulsions the student may have.
2. Let the student know that he or she is safe in your classroom and that you will not embarrass him or her in front of peers.
3. Provide as much positive recognition as possible.
4. Before giving an assignment, determine what might trigger a negative reaction. If you believe it might, think of a different way for the student to show that knowledge of the material.
5. Talk with the student privately when the student is showing difficulty with an assignment to determine how you can best meet his or her needs.
6. Break academic assignments down into small steps, so the student is not overwhelmed.
7. Provide appropriate accommodations including allowing additional time to complete a task or allowing the student to conduct their ritual.
8. Capitalize on the strengths and interests of the student.
9. Talk with your social worker/psychologist to gain their insight into the specific triggers that might be upsetting to the student.
10. Talk with parents to gain their insight into what they have found successful with their child.

Creative Connections

Visualization Art

Visualization techniques can be helpful for children experiencing anxiety. This creative connection will provide some easy exercises for children from pre-K to high school, utilizing creativity.

Setting the Stage

This is a fun exercise that starts with an environment in which all children should feel safe. Have the students gather into a circle or an arrangement in which they will be collectively focused. With some children, this may be in a circle on the floor, a circle of chairs, or sitting at their desks facing the teacher. Sometimes it may be even possible to dim the lights. Again, be mindful of all students.

Part 1: Storytelling

The teacher will tell a story or read a short story to the children. One such short story might be *Marigolds* by Eugene Collier (1969/1994). The story should be rich in descriptive detail and age appropriate. Having said that, many teenagers do love having their favorite children's book read to them. Be sure to use voice inflections and facial expressions. Have a copy of the story available for any student to reread.

Part 2: Student Creation

Pre-K to Grade Three

Ask the children to close their eyes and think about the story. Have them describe the story by making a piece of art that depicts the story. It could be a crayon drawing, a playdough sculpture, or a collage using tactile materials that you provide (such as dry macaroni, beans, different textured fabric, and yarn scraps). You might choose to ask them to "act out the story," dance, or you could ask them to verbally describe the setting of the story, or the characters. For these young students with shorter attention spans, this would be a short exercise, perhaps about 15–20 minutes. For the "speedy" children who rush through assignments, the teacher might prompt the children to add particular details.

Grades Three to Six

Have the students think about the story, how they would describe the characters, the setting, the plot of the story, or the feelings conveyed by the story. For this age group, the art project should take a little longer to complete, as one would expect more detail and proficiency in using the chosen materials. Visual art projects might include tempera or watercolor paintings, clay sculptures, collages, cartoons, or comic books. Students could also be given a choice of creating and presenting a poem, rap, song, or dance to interpret the story.

Grades Seven to 12

The project for the students in this age group would be considered a unit project. The students would be asked to create a work of art that explores in depth the plot, characters, setting, and emotional feelings of the story. They might be given a choice of media in which to work. For visual arts, you might provide, tempera paint, watercolors, acrylic paint, pastels, clay, or sculpture materials. They may choose to design comic books or graphic novels. Students may also be permitted to choose to create and present a poem, play, rap, song, dance, or video representation of the story.

Rituals: The Art of the Ritual

This creative activity focuses on the art of ritual, helping not only the anxious child, but provides all classmates an opportunity to recognize the value in rituals. Children who experience anxiety often feel a loss of control in academic and social settings. Rituals commemorate the important people and events in our lives and can result in an increased sense of comfort, balance, and strength.

Brainstorm: Ask students to define or give examples of rituals. Some rituals are short and only take a few minutes. Others may take days or months. Students may share rituals in their own lives, including celebrating birthdays, holidays, anniversaries, religious events, or other cultural or personal events.

Connect by Introducing Rituals from Multiple Cultures: Although each tribe differs, many Native American rituals include ceremonial dance, chanting, and singing. Some wear face paint and elaborate clothing adorned with furs, feathers, or colored and metallic beads. Some African cultures use ceremonial drumming or instrumental rhythms and often use masks to represent beliefs or status, or engage in ceremonial rituals to communicate the cyclical nature of life. One of the rituals of the Aboriginal people of Australia is a re-enactment of stories of mythical beings. Some musicians engage in personal rituals to help them prepare for a performance. For example, prior to every one of his concerts, Robert Plant, singer and guitar player, drinks a mug of hot tea. Singer-songwriter Rihanna gathers with her backup dancers and musicians to form a circle for moment of prayer. Olympic swimmer Michael Phelps listens to music on his headset to remain calm before each event, then takes off his headphones, steps up to the pool, and swings his arms three times. Even athletic teams have rituals, such as gathering in a huddle for a final word of inspiration prior to the start of a game. Some studies indicate that an individual's pre-performance ritual can reduce stress and increase sense of control. Prior to taking a test or engaging in a stressful task, try one of these sample pre-performance rituals: draw feelings, quietly hum, silently repeat a positive phrase, count to 10, or take five deep breaths.

Reflect and Write: Students should think of a unique, special ritual in which they and/or their loved ones engage and write a paragraph describing this event. Who is there? What happens? When does this ritual take place? Is there music? Dancing? Food? Why is this ritual significant to you?

Present or Perform: Students share their ritual with the class using visual or performing arts. Will you work independently or as a group? Will you create a painting or sculpture that visually communicates to the viewer the specifics of your ritual? Will you write and perform a dance, song, or play? Plan your presentation. What supplies will you need to create and present/perform? How much time will you need to create? How much time will you need to effectively present or perform to the class?

Evaluation: What are rituals? What are my rituals? Why are rituals important?

KEY TAKEAWAYS

♦ Anxiety disorders do have an impact on academic performance and can occur at a very early age.

♦ Students may not be motivated to change because they feel a sense of hopelessness and have a poor self-concept.

- Children with SAD are at high risk of dropping out of school.

- Worry is the key factor in students exhibiting anxiety.

- Students with OCD may have rituals they must conduct before they can do an academic task.

REFERENCES

Anila, M., & Dhanalakshmi, D. (2016). Mindfulness based stress reduction for reducing anxiety, enhancing self-control and improving academic performance among adolescent students. *Indian Journal of Positive Psychology, 7(4)*, 390–397.

Carey, E., Devine, A., Hill, F., & Szucs, D. (2017). Differentiating anxiety forms and their role in academic performance from primary to secondary school. *PLoS ONE, 12(3)*, E0174418.

Cargnelutti, E., Tomasetto, C., & Passolunghi, M. (2017). How is anxiety related to math performance in young students? A longitudinal study of grade 2 to grade 3 children. *Cognition and Emotion, 31(4)*, 755–764.

Collier, E. W. (1969/1994). Marigolds. In J. A. Hamer & M. J. Hamer (Eds.), *Centers of the self* (pp. 228–236). New York, NY: Hill and Wang.

Connor, M. J. (2003). Pupil stress and standard assessment tasks (SATs) an update. *Emotional and Behavioural Difficulties, 8*, 101–107.

Eum, K., & Rice, K. (2011). Test anxiety, perfectionism, goal orientation, and academic performance. *Anxiety, Stress and Coping, 24(2)*, 167–178.

Gagan, J., Wozniak, J., Petty, C., Vivas, F., Yorks, D., Biederman, J., & Geller, D. (2010). Clinical characteristics of comorbid obsessive-compulsive disorder and bipolar disorder in children and adolescents. *Bipolar Disorders, 12*, 185–195.

Huberty, T. (2009). Interventions for internalizing disorders. In A. Akin-Little, S. Little, M. Bray, & T. Kehle (Eds.), *Behavioral interventions in schools: Evidence-based positive strategies* (pp. 281–296). Washington, DC: American Psychological Association.

Killu, K., & Crundwell, R. (2016). Students with anxiety in the classroom: Educational accommodations and interventions. *Beyond Behavior, 25(2),* 30–40.

Nail, J., Christofferson, J., Ginsburg, G., Drake, K., Kendall, P., McCracken, J., Birmaher, B., Walkup, J., Compton, S., Keeton, C., & Sakolsky, D. (2015). Academic involvement and impact of treatments among youth with anxiety disorders. *Child & Youth Care Forum, 44,* 327–342.

Putwain, D. (2007). Test anxiety in UK schoolchildren: Prevalence and demographic patterns. *British Journal of Educational Psychology, 77,* 579–593.

Rice, K., & Ashby, J. (2007). An efficient method for classifying perfectionists. *Journal of Counseling Psychology, 54,* 72–85.

Sarason, I. (1988). Anxiety, self-preoccupation and attention. *Anxiety Research, 1,* 3–7.

Scharfstein, L., & Beidel, D. (2015). Social skills and social acceptance in children with anxiety disorders. *Journal of Clinical Child and Adolescent Psychology, 44(5),* 826–838.

Shafran, R. (2001). Obsessive-compulsive disorder in children and adolescents. *Child Psychology and Psychiatry Review, 6(2),* 50–58.

Skryabina, E., Taylor, G., & Stallard, P. (2016). Effect of a universal anxiety prevention programme (FRIENDS) on children's academic performance: Results from a randomized controlled trial. *Journal of Child Psychology and Psychiatry, 57(11),* 1297–1307.

Soohinda, G., & Sampath, H. (2016). Social phobia among school students—Prevalence, demographic correlates and socio-academic impairment. *Journal Indian Association for Child and Adolescent Mental Health, 12(3),* 211–229.

Tochkov, K. (2011). How far have we come in understanding obsessive-compulsive disorder in children and adolescents. *Annals of Psychotherapy and Integrative Health, 14(3),* 18–28.

Von Der Embse, N., & Hasson, R. (2012). Test anxiety and high-stakes test performance between school settings: Implications for educators. *Preventing School Failure, 56(3),* 180–187.

Weidle, B., & Skarphedinsson, G. (2016). Treatment of a child with obsessive-compulsive disorder with limited motivation: Course and outcome of cognitive-behavior therapy. *Journal of Clinical Psychology, 72(11),* 1139–1151.

PART II
An Overview of Effective Behavioral Interventions

7

Behavioral Management
Beginning with Functional Assessments

They say I worry too much. I try not to. I do freak out
sometimes. Well, a lot. I try so hard. What is wrong with
me?

Student, Age 13

LIVE FROM THE CLASSROOM

Mrs. Cunningham has taught students with emotional and
behavioral disorders in special education for 10 years. She has
much experience conducting functional behavioral assessments
(FBAs) with students. She believes that it is important to understand the antecedents that occur before the inappropriate behavior is exhibited. This year she is working with Mrs. Jentzen, a
sixth-grade teacher. Mrs. Jentzen has been collecting data about
one of her students, Erin, and has asked Mrs. Cunningham to
review it. Mrs. Jentzen has recorded excellent data; however, as
they review the logs, they are puzzled by the recorded behaviors.
"Erin starts crying and refuses to do her work" stymies them—
they cannot pinpoint an antecedent. Erin seems to start crying at

the beginning of the day and it does not appear that anything has caused the crying. They are confused and decide that they have to do a more thorough functional assessment, searching for some non-observable antecedents that they are missing.

It is more difficult to conduct a functional assessment for a student who has internalizing problems such as anxiety. Pinpointing an antecedent that triggered the behavior for a student with an externalizing problem is less difficult to do; with an internalizing problem, what may be bothering the student is not easily observed. It may not be possible to determine the triggers for the behavior.

The concept of analyzing the function of the behavior to determine appropriate interventions, with many variations, has been around for many years. Conducting an FBA can lead to more successful behavior changes (Scott & Alter, 2017).

This chapter discusses the steps of the functional assessment and provides strategies for conducting one with students who have anxiety disorders. To conduct a successful FBA, not only is the focus on observable antecedents, but non-observable antecedents as well.

Components of FBAs

Collecting Data

Chapter 4 of this book discusses the importance of collecting data and keeping records when witnessing signs and symptoms of anxiety. Keeping logs of observations of student behavior on a daily basis is important in determining patterns and understanding why a student is exhibiting unusual behaviors.

In documenting what is observed, Sink and Igelman (2004) advise that observable signs be described, such as shaking, crying, or withdrawal; the day and time those signs were observed; and where they occurred.

Dunlap and Kern (2018) describe the first step in a functional assessment as "descriptive data collection including interviews and direct observations intended to reveal environmental variables associated with especially high and low rates of a target behavior" (p. 316).

Creating a functional assessment requires good detective work. In conducting direct observations, study the needs of the child, watch what triggers may upset him or her, what problematic behaviors are demonstrated, and what results from these behaviors. Teachers have to think functionally in the pursuit of the underlying causes of student behavior, looking for patterns of behavior, gathering data, and hypothesizing what might be happening that is resulting in the behavior. This will be discussed further in the ABCs of FBAs section below.

Sharing this data with the social worker, school psychologist, school nurse, or counselor may allow patterns to be discerned that a teacher cannot see. Good functional assessment is a team effort; the educator is an integral part of that team by keeping data and working with the others to assist the student by figuring out why the student is engaging in some behaviors.

The reasons for the behaviors of students with anxiety are complex. It cannot be assumed that they are engaging in behaviors for one reason alone. There may be multiple factors involved. Children with anxiety often respond in the only way they know how; uncovering why they are behaving in these ways can help them change their behavior. Behavior is communication and the question is what is the student trying to communicate? This requires the teacher not only keeps watch and observes the student but also listens. Students may talk about what bothers them. Remember, the student probably wants to control their own behavior but cannot. Interviewing the student and listening to their perceptions about their behavior is essential.

A teacher may interview others who teach/work with the student within the school, including the social worker, psychologist, counselor, other school staff, bus driver, or cafeteria workers to see how the student handles situations in those settings.

What types of behaviors are the parent(s) seeing at home? More will be said about this in Chapter 11, but remember, when talking with a parent, to adopt an attitude of partnership, not blame. Ask parents to work as part of a team to meet their child's needs.

Interventions are superior when they are based on a functional assessment. More research is needed in the area of utilizing FBAs with students with anxiety disorders: More needs to be learned about how those anxiety disorders are functionally related to environmental events (Dunlap & Kern, 2018). Effective FBAs require ongoing observations of behavior (Scott & Cooper, 2017).

It is promising for those teaching in classrooms that, with assistance and/or training by those skilled in this area, the functions of behavior can be determined. Descriptive observations by teachers can make a positive difference for students (Lewis, Mitchell, Harvey, Green, & McKenzie, 2015).

The ABCs of FBAs

A description of the functional assessment process means looking at the ABCs of FBAs. "Antecedents" refer to what happened before the "Behavior" actually occurred, and "Consequences" are what happened after the behavior.

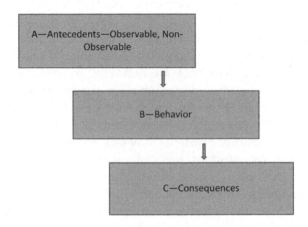

A Is for Antecedents—Observable and Non-Observable

When Jeremy was told to put his reading book away, he yelled "no" and threw the book on the floor. The teacher then told him to go to the office. This is an observable behavior and an observable consequence: This is exactly what occurred. However, with students who have anxiety disorders, have experienced trauma, or have obsessive-compulsive disorders, there may be a non-observable antecedent. For a child with anxiety, the non-observable antecedent may be fear because the child knows that it is time for math and is afraid of failure. For a child who has experienced trauma, the non-observable antecedent may be that the student was reading something reminiscent of that trauma and has become upset. The antecedent to becoming upset appeared to be about putting the book away when, in reality, the student was upset because of the content of the reading. For a child with obsessive-compulsive disorder, the student may need to engage in a ritual such as reading the entire chapter before putting a book away.

Emotional dysregulation, the inability of a person to act within the range of conventionally accepted emotive responses to external stimuli, is one of the key factors in anxiety disorders (Carthy, Horesh, Apter, & Gross, 2010; New Health Adviser for Daily Health Care, 2018). An antecedent may not be recognizable, but it demonstrates its importance when a student is asked to engage in a new task and the student refuses to do the task or leaves the room. The new task may be seen as the antecedent, but the non-observable antecedent may be the emotional dysregulation of the student: They perceive the new task as a threat to them. Because of the complexity of the needs of these students and their internalizing problems, educators cannot look just at what is seen. Is there a non-observable antecedent because the student is internalizing the nature of the challenges they face? Jumping to conclusions does not work; delving deeper is the answer.

Previous chapters have discussed children with anxiety disorders who display cognitive inflexibility; reluctance to change from one task to another. Understanding the specificity of anxiety disorder gives teachers better insight into the antecedents.

As Scott and Cooper (2017) state, "An FBA becomes complex when an individual's behavior appears to have no observable relationship with the environment" (p. 101). This may be for one of two reasons: The behavior is due to internal processes, or with students whose behaviors appear to be unrelated to the environment, in reality the complexities of the environment are too difficult to observe or isolate. Environmental antecedents may be very difficult to determine. Observations have to take place over a period of time. If the behavior has not been observed on a number of occasions, it is impossible to develop a hypothesis about the function.

B Is for Behavior

Problem behavior has been defined to include any response that is targeted for a reduction in its frequency, intensity, or duration of occurrence (Anderson, Rodriguez, & Campbell, 2015).

When observing a behavior and recording a description, the behavior should be described so that anyone could understand it. Johns (2018) uses MOO as an acronym to describe the components of writing about behavior: Every behavioral description should be written so that it is Measurable, Observable, and Objective.

A behavior written in MOO terms might include the following:

1. When given a math-independent assignment at his grade level, Matt puts his head down on his desk three out of four times and does not attempt the task.
2. When Maria walks down the hall during change of classes, she always covers her ears and does not speak to anyone.
3. When Frankie is asked to return to his desk after a short break, he instead goes over to the book-shelf, examines books, and must be redirected by the teacher at least 75% of the time.
4. When Arrie is presented with a transition task where he has to move from his reading work to his math work at the third-grade level, she cries for 10 minutes.
5. The description of these behaviors is clear. A stranger would understand the problem behavior because the records of these behaviors are measurable, observable, and objective.

The following are some non-MOO examples of behavioral descriptions:

1. Maria seems to be in another world.
2. Georgio won't follow my directions.
3. Isla refuses to work.

These statements do not tell a stranger enough about a student. What does it mean in behavioral terms for Maria to be in another world? Does it mean that she is putting her head down on her desk during reading or does it mean that she is not providing an answer to the teacher when the teacher calls on her during math? When the observation is that Georgio will not follow directions, the question is what type of directions? Are they one step or complicated, and is this behavior occurring in all situations or just in one subject? In what subject(s) is Isla refusing to work?

Defining behavior in MOO terms helps evaluate where the student currently is and what improvements are desired. Maybe

Isla, in third grade, is currently completing math work at the fifth-grade level, but only after her teacher redirects her 50% of the time? But more likely, she is in third grade and must be redirected 50% of the time by her teacher to finish her third-grade math.

Once the behavior is defined, the "fair pair" or desired replacement behavior can be defined. Thus, determining the opposite appropriate behavior—the fair pair—is the next task. In Isla's case, completing a third-grade math assignment at the third-grade level with her teacher's redirection 75% of the time may be the goal.

C Is for Consequences

When problem behaviors continue to occur, it is likely that the consequences of the behavior cause the problem behavior to occur again in the future. In Jeremy's situation, where he was told to put a book away, he yelled "no" and threw it on the floor, the consequence was that he escaped the environment. He was sent out of the classroom to the office. The occurrence of the problem behavior increases the likelihood that the same consequence will happen again, and thus a specific consequence can result in the behavior occurring over and over again.

Functions of Behavior

All behavior is driven by a purpose or, in some cases, two or three purposes. There are three broad functions of behaviors: access, escape/avoidance, and sensory needs.

Access

Children need attention. A number of students engage in certain behaviors to gain attention from teachers or peers. It may not matter whether the attention is positive or negative, as long as they receive some type of attention. Educators should look for positive behaviors that the child displays and recognize them for those behaviors rather than the negative ones.

At times, the need for access to attention is a cry for help. The child needs comfort from an adult or acceptance from peers. They do not know how to get this attention in any other way other than engaging in inappropriate behavior. The student needing attention will do whatever is required to get that attention.

A student may also be involved in non-acceptable behavior because they have a need to control specific situations. They want power in a situation and will do whatever they see as a method to get that power (Johns, 2018).

Escape/Avoidance

When demands are present in the antecedents, such as making a request for a student to do something, escape tends to be the function of the behavior. For students with anxiety disorders, if they are presented with a task that they feel threatened by and they cannot regulate their emotions, they will want to escape. They may have difficulty paying attention to a task over a specific period of time, or difficulty with cognitive flexibility when they are expected to move from one task to another. They, therefore, may avoid tasks that are too lengthy or will avoid transitioning to another activity. Children with anxiety have a high reliance on avoidance. Avoidance prevents the emergence of an uncomfortably intense experience of anxiety (Carthy, Horesh, Apter, & Gross, 2010).

Sensory

Some students will self-stimulate when in overcrowded areas or in areas where there is a lot of noise (Arora & Saldivar, 2013). They may begin rocking or moving their hands back and forth in front of their faces. Such responses refer to either hypersensitivity or hyposensitivity to stimuli in the environment. If a child is bothered by loud noises, he is overly sensitive—hypersensitive. A child exhibits hyposensitivity to the environment where there are activities surrounding them, yet they do not respond at all to the stimuli and/or self-stimulate. Students who are hyposensitive may need more stimulation and therefore may self-stimulate.

Anxiety and insistence on sameness commonly co-occur in children with autism. Black et al. (2017) studied 79 children, with autism and typically developing, to examine the relationship between anxiety and a child's insistence on sameness. In children with autism, parents reported that 67% of the time self-stimulation mediated the relationship between symptoms of a phobia and the child's insistence on sameness. The parents of children with autism with separation anxiety reported that 57% of the time self-stimulation balanced the relationship between this anxiety and insistence on sameness. In typically developing children, no relationship between self-stimulation and social anxiety problems was reported. Rigidity that is associated with insistence on sameness has been thought to compound stress, but it can also function as a coping mechanism. Sensory hypersensitivity can assist in explaining the co-occurrence of both anxiety and insistence on sameness in children with autism. Specific phobias have been found to be related to hypersensitivity (Kerns et al., 2014).

There is a link between maladaptive sensory responsiveness and various mental health disorders and interpersonal difficulties; a link that can occur between sensory sensitivity and anxiety. Children can overestimate threatening stimuli, and this can influence behavior. Children with hypersensitivity to tactile sensations initiated by others may show high anxiety levels. Children may seek sensory stimulation, may avoid sensory stimulation, or may show low registration of sensory stimuli (Levit-Binnum, Szepsenwol, Stern-Ellran, & Engel-Yeger, 2014).

Anxiety can contribute to sensory over-responsivity where the child is hypervigilant about specific types of sensory stimulus. When children are hypervigilant, they are scanning the environment and may be more likely to perceive aversive sensory stimuli. The threat-based emotional regulation that is associated with anxiety makes it difficult for the child to regulate their responses to the stimuli (Green & Ben-Sasson, 2010).

Other Factors

In a functional assessment, additional factors such as medical concerns, cultural issues, and environmental factors may be significant reasons for the behaviors being exhibited. When children are on medication for anxiety or other reasons, the medications may not be appropriate, may be an over or under dosage, or may produce side effects that might explain changes in behavior.

The child's culture may play a role in the student's behavior. One high school student had moved to a continental state from Puerto Rico. He was bright and could speak English but had to work hard to utilize correct grammar. He started showing significant signs of anxiety, specifically shaking and withdrawal. Educators suspected anxiety issues. In exploring the student's schedule, it was found that he was enrolled in a high school English class where the teacher expected six writing assignments per week. The student was overwhelmed by these assignments. Once reassigned to another class and provided with additional assistance in writing, his behaviors potentially related to anxiety disappeared.

When students are afraid to come to school, they may have been exposed to bullying by peers or staff. The thought of returning to a setting where bullying occurred is frightening to the child. One student with autism spectrum disorders was grabbed by the arm by a building principal. The student was so traumatized by this event that he would not go back to school. He was afraid of the building principal. The mother eventually homeschooled him. Ten years later and having been provided several years of counseling, they still cannot drive by that school without the young man having a panic attack.

How Functional Assessments Can Result in Meaningful Behavior Interventions

When teachers think functionally, they are more likely to understand the multitude of variables that may be occurring. How can they change the antecedents, the consequences of the behavior, and/or the environmental variables that may make a positive difference for the student? Dunlap and Kerns (2018) found that effective teachers, who think about behavior in terms of function, can create positive and constructive ways to help students through well-planned instruction and changes in the environment. Functional assessments should culminate in meaningful behavior interventions.

Functional assessments should involve the systematic altering of environmental factors based on the observations and interviews the teacher has done (Flanagan & DeBar, 2018). When educators have collected data, they can describe the variables and incorporate them into their planning, resulting in more appropriate behaviors. A behavior intervention plan includes antecedent and consequence manipulations, i.e., how the child is attempting to control the situation, as well as methods for teaching a replacement behavior (Scott & Cooper, 2017).

This chapter discusses behaviors that students exhibit that may be prompted or made worse by anxiety. Minahan and Rappaport (2012) call for teachers to learn how to create prescribed behavioral intervention plans to address anxiety and instruction in the skills needed to learn more effective coping strategies and accommodations.

The remaining chapters of Part II contain more information and strategies about how to change antecedents and consequences, and how to teach replacement behaviors.

TEN TEACHING TIPS

1. Teachers can document observed patterns of behaviors in students, including noting the specific behaviors, where they occur, and when they occur.
2. Interviewing the student, families, and other school personnel helps the teacher to gather as much assessment information as possible.
3. Working as a team member helps to determine the possible antecedents and possible functions of the behavior.
4. Utilizing information in an FBA, teachers can determine appropriate interventions for the behavior intervention plan.
5. Teachers should work to prevent negative antecedents within their control.
6. Examine the use of consequences when a child misbehaves to avoid escalation of the behavior.
7. Try to determine whether the function of the child's behavior is access to attention. If so, the teacher can provide attention when the student is engaging in appropriate behavior.
8. If a child is engaging in a specific behavior to escape or avoid a specific task, the teacher can look closely at the task and see if it can be reframed.
9. Other factors may be causing inappropriate behaviors, such as medical reasons, cultural factors, and environmental factors.
10. Avoid placing students with anxiety disorders in situations where there is a possibility of sensory overload or excessive sensory stimulation.

Creative Connections

Patterns

What are patterns? A pattern is a recurring design, with elements of the pattern repeating in a predictable manner. They can be found everywhere, in every aspect of life, including in nature, music, art, history, mathematics, clothing, household goods, and sports. Even our emotions and behaviors represent patterns.

For children who experience anxiety, patterns are important; recognizing patterns can help with transitions and can provide a sense of calm. The patterns in a school day, such as knowing the transitions and repetitions of activities, can help reduce stress.

The following creative activities can be adapted for students of all ages.

Option #1—Fun with Beads

Materials

Beads in a variety of colors, sizes, shapes, and textures; pipe cleaners, string, yarn, or wire; large eyed needles (plastic or metal); scissors, pliers/wire cutters, assorted jewelry findings, and fasteners.

Directions

For younger students, use pipe cleaners and large beads to create simple patterns. Ask students what makes a pattern? A pattern can be created by repeating two or three differently colored beads, or alternating different shapes, sizes, or textures. Students can create a simple beaded pattern by choosing two colors and stringing them in groups, such as one small red bead followed by two large green beads, and repeating with one small red bead, two large green beads, and so on until the desired length of the bracelet is formed. Twist the pipe cleaner together at the end, creating a circular bracelet.

Allow older students to choose from a larger variety of materials to create more complex patterns. Guide the students to determine an identical segment with the beads, repeating the pattern several times, and then incorporate a transition bead between each pattern segment. The students can choose to fashion the beads into a variety of products: bracelets, necklaces, key chains, light/fan pulls, or zipper pulls.

Option #2—Charting Patterns

Have students look for patterns in the school day. Teach them to create a chart to record these patterns in the sequence in which they occur. They can chart weather patterns, patterns in attendance, in mathematics, in music, science, history, and language.

Help students become aware of their own patterns of behavior and emotions. Students can create a personal symbol for their chart to identify each feeling, perhaps a smiley face for happy emotions, or a thumbs-down for feeling sad. This can be done on paper or computer.

After the students have recorded feelings and behaviors over time, they can engage in reflection. What patterns emerged? What happened right before a negative emotion or negative behavior?

What happened right before a positive emotion or behavior? What can we learn about ourselves and our reactions to an environment? What changes, if any would you like to make?

Option #3—Before and After

Sequencing is an important skill and is included in all academic standards. This aesthetic activity guides students of all ages to explore a sequence of events by looking at art photographs. Photographs can be obtained online from various museums or galleries, or students can be assigned to take photographs in their school, home, or community.

Directions

Students will look at a photograph and share their interpretations with the whole class by creating a narrative. Prompts to encourage discussion might include: What is happening in this photograph? What do you think might have happened before this incident? What do you see that makes you think that? What do you think will happen next and why? Students may brainstorm very different scenarios, and all are acceptable.

KEY TAKEAWAYS

- Determining the antecedents of behavior requires the investigation of both observable and non-observable triggers.

- It is more difficult to conduct an FBA with students with internalizing anxiety than with those who externalize their behaviors.

- Consequences that occur because of an inappropriate behavior may be encouraging or maintaining that behavior.

- Functions of behavior can include access or attention, escape/avoidance, or sensory needs.

- Information gathered from functional assessments should be utilized to create a positive behavior intervention plan.

REFERENCES

Anderson, C., Rodriguez, B., & Campbell, A. (2015). Functional behavior assessment in schools: Current status and future directions. *Journal of Behavioral Education, 24*, 338–371.

Arora, T., & Saldivar, B. (2013). A case study of a high school student with autism including a functional analysis assessment intervention to target anxiety and perseveration. *Journal of Instructional Psychology, 40(3)*, 61–74.

Black, K., Stevenson, R., Segers, M., Ncube, B., Sun, S., Philipp-Muller, A., Bebko, J., Barense, M., & Ferber, S. (2017). Linking anxiety and insistence on sameness in autistic children: The role of sensory hypersensitivity. *Journal of Autism and Developmental Disorders, 47*, 2459–2470.

Carthy, T., Horesh, N., Apter, A., & Gross, J. (2010). Patterns of emotional reactivity and regulation in children with anxiety disorders. *Journal of Psychopathology and Behavioral Assessment, 32*, 23–36.

Dunlap, G., & Kern, L. (2018). Perspectives on functional assessment. *Behavioral Disorders, 43(2)*, 316–321.

Green, S., & Ben-Sasson. (2010). Anxiety disorders and sensory over-responsivity in children with autism spectrum disorders: Is there a causal relationship? *Journal of Autism and Developmental Disabilities, 40*, 1495–1504.

Flanagan, T., & DeBar, R. (2018). Trial-based functional analyses with a student identified with an emotional and behavioral disorder. *Behavioral Disorders, 43(4)*, 423–435.

Johns, B. (2018). *Techniques for managing verbally and physically aggressive students* (4th ed.). Austin, TX: Pro-Ed.

Kerns, C., Kendall, P., Berry, L., Souders, M., Franklin, M., Schultz, R., Miller, J., & Herrington, J. (2014). Traditional and atypical presentations of anxiety in youth with autism spectrum disorder. *Journal of Autism and Developmental Disorders, 44(11)*, 2851–2861.

Levit-Binnum, N., Szepsenwol, O., Stern-Ellran, K., & Engel-Yeger, B. (2014). The relationship between sensory responsiveness profiles, attachment orientations, and anxiety symptoms. *Australian Journal of Psychology, 66*, 233–240.

Lewis, T., Mitchell, B., Harvey, K., Green, A., & McKenzie, J. (2015). A comparison of functional behavioral assessment and functional analysis methodology among students with mild disabilities. *Behavioral Disorders, 41(1)*, 5–20.

Minahan, J., & Rappaport, N. (2012). Anxiety in students: A hidden culprit in behavior issues. *Kappan, 94(4)*, 34–39.

New Health Adviser for Daily Health Care. (2018). *Emotional dysfunction.* Retrieved October 16, 2018 from www.newhealthadvisor.com/EmotionalDysfunction.html

Scott, T., & Alter, P. (2017). Examining the case for functional behavior assessment as an evidence-based practice for students with emotional and behavioral disorders in general education classrooms. *Preventing School Failure, 61(1)*, 80–93.

Scott, T., & Cooper, J. (2017). Functional behavior assessment and function-based intervention planning: Considering the simple logic of the process. *Beyond Behavior, 26(3)*, 101–104.

Sink, C., & Igelman, C. (2004). Anxiety disorders. In F. Kline & L. Silver (Eds.), *The educator's guide to mental health issues in the classroom* (pp. 171–191). Baltimore, MD: Brookes Publishing.

8

Preventive Interventions

I try not to feed the worry bug, but it keeps growing.

Six Year Old

LIVE FROM THE CLASSROOM

Ms. Barber took a position as a teacher of students with autism in a new school district. This would be her first experience in a special education classroom. Previously, she had taught fourth grade. She and the school social worker had always gone to the homes of the students before school started because many of her students were anxious about having a new teacher and coming into a new classroom. At her new school, she knew that it would be even more important to do home visits with her students because students with autism often have high levels of anxiety, especially when given a new situation. She asked the principal whether this was acceptable protocol in the school. The principal told her that the social worker in the school used to do home visits but quit doing them because some of the students lived in neighborhoods that were not safe. He added that, if she wanted to do them, it was okay with him, but she needed to recognize the potential risks. She then asked the social worker to accompany her on the home visits prior to the start of the school year. The social worker was happy to go with her; the social worker said that she hadn't been able to get any other teachers to go with her before, and she was afraid to go alone.

Ms. Barber believed that it was important to relieve student anxiety about a new teacher by meeting the students before school started. She contacted the parents and asked if she could come to the home to meet their child or if the parents wanted to meet with her at another location. She had learned that some parents were embarrassed by the condition of their home, and she wanted to respect their privacy. As it happened, all of the parents were grateful that she would come to their homes. She and the social worker really enjoyed the visits and getting to meet the families. She also invited them to come and visit her at school before the school year started so they could see the classroom. The parents were grateful because they had been worried about their children having a new teacher and how they would react. Ms. Barber; the social worker; the parents; and, most importantly, the students got off to a good start, and the level of anxiety was reduced for all.

This chapter provides a whole array of strategies like those Ms. Barber used to reduce anxiety on the part of the students. When students get upset because of their anxiety, a teacher can utilize effective de-escalation techniques.

Every day, educators struggle to achieve balance between students who face challenges and those who do not need as much individual attention. Competent educators are reflective and carefully examine how much time they are working with students. When teachers believe that they are not providing enough attention to the other students within the classroom, they should seek additional assistance from their administration or other support personnel.

Preventive Strategies

Talking to children in a supportive and non-threatening manner can reduce their anxiety and provide them with a classroom that is a comfort zone. This forms the basis for building positive relationships.

Building Relationships

When Ms. Barber went to the homes of her prospective students, she was building relationships with the students and their families. She sent the message that she cared enough about them to get to know them and reduced her students' anxiety about having a new teacher and a new environment.

A promise made to a student must be kept: Students who are anxious are very vigilant, and if they know that they can count on an educator to do what was discussed, their anxiety levels can be reduced.

It is often the little things that go a long way in building positive relationships with students. Here are a few:

♦ Use the child's name and greet him as he enters the classroom.

♦ Have a warm and friendly smile on your face when the student comes in.

♦ Let the student know that you are happy to see him.

♦ Compliment the student for something he is wearing or for his smile.

♦ Know the student's interests and ask about them (e.g., "Hey, what did you think about that basketball game last night?")

Students listen to adults when they have made a connection with them. They connect for protection and for gratification. The teacher has to convey an attitude of respect, care, enhancement, and affirmation (Wood & Long, 1991).

Besides building relationships within school, plan a "relationship culture" (McGrath & Noble, 2010, p. 81). This includes the intentional promotion of positive peer relationships. Students need to feel accepted by teachers and peers. Teach students how to engage in cooperative learning and positively reinforce them for doing so; teach social skills; and provide opportunities for multi-age sporting, drama, music, and art activities. Lunchtime clubs are also important. Students with anxiety may be at risk for being bullied and rejected by other students; educators need to make the well-being of their students a top priority (McGrath & Noble, 2010).

Building Structure and Routine

Students should be provided with a specific schedule and clear expectations. In secondary school where students are expected to move from one class to another, they should be provided with a schedule that they can carry in a purse or backpack. Schedule changes can occur because of weather emergencies, school pictures, hearing and vision screening, or water main break. Prepare students for those changes. Once students are in the classroom, the specific schedule for the day should be posted for the students to visually see, and it should be reviewed verbally with them.

Students with anxiety may also need checklists for assignments so that they know what they are supposed to do. Some students have difficulty proofreading their work so they may need to be provided a checklist to help them remember to put their name on their paper, check for spelling, and check for capitalization. What materials need to go home at the end of the day? The teacher can write down what the child needs, and the student can locate the items, check them off the list, and put them in the backpack (Swanson, 2005).

Some students may also need small cards that give them step-by-step directions for daily tasks. These cards can be kept at the table for all students to use, or specific cards can be personalized to meet the needs of an individual.

Prepare students for transitioning between activities. The educator can say, "We have five minutes left to finish our writing assignment." A variety of visual timers, without the auditory component, are available, so students can visually see how much time they have left. Sound timers may result in anxiety for some students because they are spending their time anticipating the unpleasant noise that is about to occur.

Building a Classroom Management System that Supports Students

Some teachers use motivational systems designed to recognize students who do well and keep track of students who do not do well. For students who are anxious, some systems can create an environment where children feel on alert all day for fear they are going to do something wrong. A common example used in some schools is the red, yellow, green light. If you are doing well, you stay on the green light. If you begin to have behavioral issues, you are on the yellow caution light, and if you do something wrong, you get the red light. This system may be effective for some students, but before using it with children who have anxiety, a teacher may want to investigate whether the system results in a higher level of anxiety for the student.

Another popular system is referred to as response cost. Students earn points or tokens for positive behavior. If students engage in inappropriate behavior, then points are taken away. This system may be too stressful for some students with anxiety, and a better approach may be to establish a system where students earn points for appropriate behaviors but do not lose for inappropriate behaviors.

At all times, students need to know the expectations for their behavior and be taught the logical consequences for inappropriate behavior. If the student throws his food on the floor, the student should know in advance that he or she will have to clean the food off the floor (Johns, 2018a). There should not be surprise consequences for inappropriate behavior: A student misbehaved at recess, which resulted in the student losing recess privileges for the next week. The student had no idea this would happen when he misbehaved.

Write clear rules in positive terms. Inform students which behaviors are preferred rather than those behaviors that are inappropriate (Swanson, 2005). Students can be given prior warnings, so there will be no surprise consequences.

Building Appropriate Classroom Assignments

The previous chapter discussed that some students with anxiety engage in inappropriate behaviors because they do not want to do a task they perceive as difficult. They are afraid of failing. If it is determined that a student is engaging in escape/avoidance behavior, then the following questions may help when planning independent tasks for these students:

1. Is the work something that the student is able to complete independently? Sometimes educators assume that students can do things that are too difficult for them.

2. Is too much work being given at one time? For a student with anxiety, giving one sheet of paper at a time rather than everything at once may help.
3. Does the student understand the directions?
4. Is there more than one set of directions on one sheet of paper? Students with anxiety can have cognitive inflexibility and have difficulty switching activities and/or switching directions.
5. Is the print too small for the student? While enlarged print is used for students who are visually impaired, it may also be appropriate for students who have anxiety because it is easier for them to read.

Asking these questions before preparing a task for some students can prevent anxiety.

When conducting large group activities, teachers can prevent confusion and stress for students by breaking down the tasks into small parts and using a multi-sensory approach that includes showing, telling, and/or hands on work.

The *I Do, We Do, You Do* approach can be effective when teachers are showing students how to do a specific assignment. Adding an extra step provides more opportunity to practice before having the students start an assignment themselves. It is I do, we do, you do with a partner or small group, and then you do. This process provides for two or more students to do a problem together, before having to do a problem alone.

Use preventive strategies in group work. For students with anxiety, it can be very stressful if the teacher tells them to pick a partner with whom to work. The students can be worried that no one will want to work with them. The teacher can alleviate stress and embarrassment for students by assigning groups with those who work together effectively.

In group discussions rather than calling on students, the teacher can utilize well-researched response card methods. This can prevent students from worrying that they will be called when they might not know the answer. There are many response card methods—stand up for yes, stay seated for no, hold up your yes card or no card up for your answer, and so on (Johns, 2015).

The teacher can give each student an individual whiteboard: When the teacher asks a question, each student writes down their answer. They then hold up the whiteboard so that the teacher can see the answers. Computer clickers (hand-held devices that allow a student to electronically respond to questions) are a form of response, and students do not know who gave which answer.

Whether calling on a student in a large group or working with a student one-on-one, provide adequate wait time, so the student has time to process the information and act. Students with anxiety worry, and that worry decreases their ability to process information quickly; the teacher should observe how long it takes a student to process and give that amount of wait time to the student.

Building a Physical Environment That Is Conducive to Learning

It is helpful to learn about the child's anxiety antecedents, make the classroom conducive to learning and as stress free as possible. Betsy is a student with social anxiety disorder, and the teacher thought she was helping by having her sit in the front of the classroom. Betsy seemed very anxious and kept looking behind her. Betsy's teacher asked her privately why she kept looking behind her. Betsy replied that she hated sitting in the front because she could not see what was behind her and that made her more nervous. Preferential seating for Betsy was seating in the back of the room rather than the front. Betsy was hypervigilant, and placing her in a location where she could see everyone lessened her anxiety.

In the previous chapter, we discussed that students may be hypersensitive to certain stimuli in the physical environment. The classroom may be too visually busy, with posters on walls, materials scattered, and multiple stations in the room for students. The lighting may be too bright. The flicker and hum of fluorescent lights may bother some students. If permitted, alternatives to those lights can be lamps, which may be calming for students. Some students are very sensitive to the noise in the environment and may need headphones.

Children who exhibit anxiety need a sense of order. Clutter should be reduced as much as possible (Swanson, 2005). A designated area for each item can help.

Some students are nervous about attending school-wide assemblies. It helps to take them into the assembly before others arrive so they can watch the other students enter.

Educators should never change the room arrangement without preparing the students. Some educators change their room around every weekend to surprise the students when they arrive on Monday. These changes can be invigorating for some students but can be very unpleasant for a student with high levels of anxiety. Knowing what to expect can reduce anxiety for those students who do not appreciate change.

De-escalation Strategies

There is documented comorbidity among children with anxiety disorders and oppositional defiant disorders (ODD), meaning that anxiety disorders and ODD often occur simultaneously. In preschoolers, anxiety disorders and ODD comorbidity range from 7% to 14%. Having anxiety disorders and ODD in later childhood can result in high negative emotionality and low inhibitory control, and potential behavioral disinhibition (Martin, Granero, Domenech, & Ezpelata, 2017). As a result, some students with anxiety disorders may become defiant or engage in hostile behaviors; some of these overt behaviors may be a result of internal fears and worries.

The first part of this chapter emphasized the importance of prevention. By controlling the variables which may result in increased anxiety and therefore overt aggressive behavior, the possibility of behavioral outbreaks may be reduced.

Avoidance of Power Struggles—Be Positive, Be Brief, Be Gone

Engaging in power struggles with students never has a good outcome. A student may begin to argue, and it is human nature to want to argue back. An effective preventive strategy for this is the Be Positive, Be Brief, Be Gone. What does this mean?

First, when a teacher wants a student to follow directions, only one step should be given. The teacher should state, "It is time to start your math." This is positive and brief. If a student is anxious, complex directions may result in increased anxiety and non-compliance. Then the teacher moves away from the student because standing over the student and hovering may make the student more anxious. When the teacher sees the student begin to work, then the teacher can return to the student to reinforce his or her efforts and offer supportive assistance. Requesting that a student start a task is more desirable than requesting that a student get all of an assignment done because starting is not as overwhelming. A request to get a lot of work done can be anxiety-provoking to a student.

Some students have a history of rejection or lack of involvement with adults. When the teacher sends the student to the office, the student may perceive that this adult does not care enough about them to try to solve the problem. In addition, the message suggests that this teacher does not have the skill to handle conflicts (Jones, Dohrn, & Dunn, 2014).

Calm Approach

The teacher is the role model for the calm approach. There is a positive ripple effect that occurs when the teacher remains calm (Jones, Dohrn, & Dunn, 2014). The teacher should always lower her voice and avoid showing tension (Johns, 2018b). The student, who may be yelling, learns that the teacher is not going to yell back and is going to stay composed. If the teacher says anything, it should be short and said slowly. Remember when the child is angry or upset, the child is not processing the information quickly and therefore any direction conveyed must be short and clear.

When asking what is bothering the student or what might help, ask an open-ended question and make sure it is a question that the student can answer. A small sticky note placed on the student's desk with a written invitation to talk when the lesson is over can be a good idea (Jones, Dohrn, & Dunn, 2014).

Educators may also adopt this motto when a student is upset and is becoming resistant—*Open up, Back up, Clam up*. What does this mean? When a student is resistant or being verbally inappropriate, he may become anxious if the teacher gets too close. Some students may wonder what the teacher has in his or her hands. The teacher should reveal open hands, back up, and keep quiet. If the teacher is not engaging in a verbal battle with the student, the student may stop the inappropriate verbal comments. In the previous chapter, we described access to attention as a possible function of behavior; if the misbehavior is to gain attention, giving the student attention for inappropriate behavior reinforces that inappropriate behavior, and the student may continue to engage in it. Use every opportunity to practice giving attention for appropriate behavior.

Privacy

When a student is upset, there are two important reasons to provide privacy. One is that it is respectful. A student should not be embarrassed in front of peers or other adults. Giving the student the option to accompany the teacher to a private area is important. They then have the opportunity to discuss what has happened privately, which increases the likelihood that the student may share valuable insight into what has occurred.

The second reason, if the student is engaging in inappropriate behavior to seek attention, is that removing the audience removes this motivation. Taking the student out of the environment reduces the opportunity to get the attention.

What does the teacher do when the student refuses to leave the classroom environment? The teacher can call for another adult to take the other students to a different room: A plan to have another adult available to stay with the others in the class, whether they stay while the teacher and child go elsewhere, or the others in the class move, should be in place as part of a crisis plan before it is required. The teacher can also provide a choice by saying to the student, "Please leave the classroom with me." If necessary, this statement can be followed with "We can either leave together, or the other class members will be leaving." Giving students a choice gives them a sense of control; some students who feel that they have no power and control benefit from that opportunity.

Supportive Verbal Strategies

When a student is talking, often it is wise for an educator to say nothing and just listen to the messages conveyed. Educators need to be supportive active listeners, listening to understand, not to respond. Do not think of your future responses, while the child is talking; just listen.

Benn (2018) advocates the use of compassionate communication, applying basic manners to build rapport with students. Saying "Please" or "Thank you" in a sincere manner shows the student respect. Saying "Is it okay if I . . ." asks the student for permission to assist them.

Use precision statements to let students know what is expected. A statement such as "We will put our math book away in two minutes" is better than saying, "Math is almost over and then we are going to move on to do our reading assignment so be sure to take your reading book out." Statements should be short, positive, and relay exactly what is to be done.

Good teachers learn to read their students. If a teacher sees that a student is becoming anxious, the teacher may want to approach the student privately and ask whether the student needs assistance or there is something that could be done to help. Avoid asking what is wrong with the student because this gives the student a negative impression. Examples of positive and supportive verbal statements can include:

♦ How can I help you with this?

♦ Let's work on this together.

♦ What can you do to follow this rule?

♦ What is it that would make you feel better?

♦ Is there someone that you would like to talk to?

♦ Could you tell me what is happening?

♦ Is there something bothering you that I can help with?

♦ Let's start on this together.

By utilizing the preventive strategies described in this chapter, the educator can provide an environment that is safe and secure for the student and will reduce the number of anxiety-related inappropriate behaviors.

TEN TEACHING TIPS

1. Build positive relationships by getting to know students' strengths and interests.
2. Create structure and routine to provide students with the assurance that they are safe in your environment.
3. Investigate your classroom management system to ensure that it is not causing anxiety for your students.
4. Review classroom assignments to determine that they are at the appropriate level, presented with clarity, and involve one direction at a time.

5. Investigate the physical arrangement of your classroom to determine whether there are any anxiety triggers.
6. Avoid power struggles with students by giving positive brief statements to students in a calm supportive manner.
7. Provide privacy to students when they are upset.
8. Engage in active listening designed to understand what the child is saying.
9. Be a role model by using positive statements and manners.
10. Look for early warning signs that a student is becoming anxious and interact with the student in a supportive manner.

Creative Connections

Affirmation Journals

Sometimes, students experience anxiety and seem to focus on negative events that may or may not exist. Keeping affirmation journals can help students transform negative thoughts and worries into positive affirmations and actions. These journals are intended to be personal and therefore all students' privacy should be respected. Do not require that students share their reflections with other students.

Use pre-made sketch journals, or students can make handmade books. A handmade book can be as simple as taking several sheets of paper, folding it down the middle, stapling on the middle line, and creating a cover for it. It can be something small they can take with them or a fancy journal that can be used long term. Older students can explore various complex bookmaking methods. Students can use pencils, markers, color pencils, or other art media to write words and/or draw their responses to a variety of prompts. Another alternative is to create collages by cutting out pertinent images and words from magazines to glue onto their journal pages.

It is helpful to create a list of prompts in advance for students to use. These prompts can stimulate students' thoughts and help turn their thoughts into positive affirmations. These statements may represent them or their lives. This list can be displayed on the board or printed on paper and given to each student to include in their journal.

Sample prompts can include: "I am _____"; "I am proud of myself when _____"; "I am most happy when _____"; "If I gave my current or past feeling a color, that color would be _____"; "I feel strong when _____"; "I am unstoppable when _____"; "Sometimes my feelings are like a monster, it looks like _____"; "I can't wait until _____"; "Something that happened yesterday that I am grateful for is _____"; "The _____ (list people, things, places) I love _____."

We Have Your Back

The goal of this activity is to change student outlook by providing bold statements of positive affirmation throughout the school. Walking down the halls between classes; using the restrooms; eating in the cafeteria; and going into certain areas of the school, such as the locker room for gym, can be fearful, leaving students feeling alone, left out, stressed out, and anxious. By providing bold visual affirmation that every student is important, recognized, and cared for, the physical space sets the mood for safety and belonging. It can also build a sense of self and proclaim to all students: "We Are with You 100% of the Way!" Such affirming messages might include: You Are Stronger Than You Think; Think Positive Be Positive; Never Give Up; A Positive Attitude Becomes Strength of Character; To Keep Your Balance, You Must Keep Moving; Where There Is No Struggle, There Is No Strength; Worrying Does Not Empty Tomorrow of Its Struggles, It Empties Today of Its Strength; Believe In Yourself Even If No One Else Does; I Am A Work In Progress and That's Okay; I Am Willing To Do What It Takes!

Student ownership can be enhanced by forming a student graffiti patrol to make sure that any vandalized affirmative messages are repaired or replaced in a timely manner.

Option 1

Banners created by the students can be hung in various areas of the school. These banners could be changed monthly or seasonally and can highlight a particular affirmation thread. *Materials:* paint, brushes, broad-tip markers, colored duct tape, roll of craft paper, sheets of fabric, water containers, and paper towels.

Option 2

Posters may be more manageable than banners for some schools but no less effective. *Materials:* poster board, cardboard, paint, paintbrushes, water containers, paper towels, markers, magazines, glue, scissors. Students can also make computerized posters.

Option 3

Murals can be painted directly on hallway walls, stairwells, doors in bathroom stalls, locker rooms, cafeteria, ceiling tiles, or any area that might be intimidating to students. Be sure to get permission before painting on any surface in the school.

Materials

Pencils for drawing the graphics prior to painting, water-based acrylic paints, brushes, water containers, paper towels, drop cloths, and aprons or smocks.

Option 4

Academic teachers and support personnel, working with the art teacher and students, can take an active role in creating the affirmative messages with the students. This will psychologically show the students an adult investment when assisting in the making of the banners, posters, or murals. Students can assume leadership in the design and therefore benefit from this type of collaborative creative work. Some adults may feel limited in their artistic ability but may enjoy serving as assistants to the student designers.

KEY TAKEAWAYS

♦ Building positive relationships with students with anxiety makes a positive difference in the student's comfort level at school.

- Preventive strategies, such as pre-planning structure and routine, investigating classroom assignments, examining behavior management systems, and arranging the physical environment to ensure security for the students, may lessen their anxiety.

- De-escalation strategies include a calm and supportive manner, and privacy for the student.

- Supportive verbal statements should be utilized.

- Teachers can reduce anxiety by learning as much about the child's triggers, planning ahead, and engaging in supportive activities.

REFERENCES

Benn, G. (2018). You don't know me like that. *Educational Leadership, 76(1)*, 20–25.

Johns, B. (2015). *15 Positive behavior strategies to increase academic success*. Thousand Oaks, CA: Corwin.

Johns, B. (2018a). *Reduction of school violence* (5th ed.). Palm Beach Gardens, FL: LRP.

Johns, B. (2018b). *Techniques for managing verbally and physically aggressive students*. Austin, TX: Pro-Ed.

Jones, V., Dohrn, E., & Dunn, C. (2014). *Creating effective programs for students with emotional and behavioral disorders*. Boston, MA: Pearson.

Martin, V., Granero, R., Domenech, J., & Ezpeleta, L. (2017). Factors related to the comorbidity between oppositional defiant disorder and anxiety disorders in preschool children. *Anxiety, Stress, and Coping, 30(2)*, 228–242.

McGrath, H., & Noble, T. (2010). Supporting positive pupil relationships: Research to practice. *Educational and Child Psychology, 27(1)*, 79–90.

Swanson, T. (2005). Provide structure for children with learning and behavior problems. *Intervention in School and Clinic, 40(3)*, 182–187.

Wood, M., & Long, N. (1991). *Life space intervention: Talking with children and youth in crisis*. Austin, TX: Pro-Ed.

9

Effective Behavioral Strategies

Sometimes when I'm preparing for a test and my anxiety gets the best of me, I like to do something like pave a walkway, 'cause it makes me focus on just this one thing, one thing that I can see my progress and I can finish. Focusing on this one thing helps me clear my head, and makes it impossible for all the worry thoughts to enter my head.

A High School Student

LIVE FROM THE CLASSROOM

Mrs. Johansen has been teaching for over 15 years in the math department at the secondary level. She has noticed that over the years, a number of her students have math anxiety when they come into her classroom. She has learned to teach them a number of coping strategies, including some to reduce anxiety and stress. As a result, most of the students who come into her classroom hating math love it by the time they complete her course.

She was recently asked by a new teacher what her secret was. She contemplated what she had done over the years to make a positive difference in the lives of her students, many of whom had come in stressed, anxious, and disenfranchised from school, and, in particular, mathematics. She wanted to give some words of wisdom to this teacher that would help him become a teacher who could also motivate and inspire his students.

As she reflected on her teaching, she realized that throughout the day, she incorporated relevant activities that connected math to everyday living so that every time one of her students asked why they had to learn something, she could explain how they would use math throughout their lives. She also incorporated self-monitoring strategies where each student charted their progress in skill areas where previously they had exhibited problems. She incorporated choices throughout her math periods. When she gave an assignment, she did not give just one assignment, she gave two or three choices, and the students could choose to do whichever one they wanted to do. She also incorporated periodic relaxation exercises as well as movement activities spread throughout the day. She would note when students needed a short break because they were getting stressed, and she would build in short relaxation and movement exercises for them. Mrs. Johansen hoped that the lessons she learned would help the new teacher.

This chapter presents an array of ideas to reduce the anxiety of the students within classrooms.

Anxiety Reduction Strategies

The ultimate goal for all students is that they become independent individuals who rely on themselves to solve their problems and to control their own behavior. Perceived competence on the part of a student is his or her perception of their ability to produce a desired outcome. This belief includes self-efficacy, i.e., involving the student's perception of their ability to deal with negative emotions and manage their internal feelings. Both external locus of control (the belief that a person's behavior is not within their control) and low self-efficacy have a strong association with youth anxiety. Low emotional self-efficacy is linked to clinically impaired levels of anxiety (Niditch & Varela, 2012). Muris (2002) showed that low self-efficacy in the social, academic, and emotional domains was related to symptoms of anxiety disorders.

It is key for teachers to stress to their students that they are in control of their emotions and that they have the ability to make choices. Throughout the day, it is important that teachers give students the opportunity to make choices and to reinforce strong decisions. When a student is becoming upset and a possibility exists that the student may lose control, the teacher can say to the student quietly, "It looks like you are upset, would you prefer to keep working or take a time-out for a few minutes and rejoin us when you feel calmer?" The teacher is giving the student two acceptable choices, and the student can decide. The teacher then reinforces the student for the choice they made.

Throughout this book, we have stressed the importance of emotional regulation. It is defined as "an individual's emotions and when and how he/she experiences and expresses them" (Abasi, Dolatshahi, Farazmand, Pourshahbaz, & Tamanaeefar, 2018, p. 161). These are processes by which students modify their emotions, either adaptively or maladaptively. Maladaptive processes are common among emotional disorders; among those disorders, generalized anxiety disorders and social anxiety disorders can co-occur. Attentional control has been found in the etiology and the continuation of anxiety disorders, both generalized anxiety and social anxiety disorders.

Transition points have been shown to create times of psychological disequilibrium and can result in increased vulnerability to psychological disturbance; however, at the same time, they can be a time for psychological growth for a student. Students have to overcome initial anxiety, break old habits, and create new coping styles (Greene & Ollendick, 1991). Previous chapters revealed that a characteristic of students with anxiety is cognitive inflexibility. They may have difficulty making transitions. As part of the self-monitoring process, teachers need to prepare students for times of transition. They can give time signals alerting students of an upcoming transition. One suggestion is to verbally announce the remaining minutes until the next activity, subject, or class. Another is to utilize a visual timer that shows the amount of time that the students have left for the current activity. Some visual timers do not utilize sound because the time ticking away may increase a student's anxiety. Teachers can also give visual cues about what is being done now and what will be done next. Holding up picture schedules or visual timer cards can alert students to the next activity. Students who accomplish a transition satisfactorily should be recognized for having done so.

Self-Monitoring

Self-monitoring is an important process for students to measure and see their own progress. Teachers can assist the student in establishing a system where they can record and monitor their own behavior to create an internal locus of control (Jones, Dohrn, & Dunn, 2004). Teachers should strive to create a visual and personal system of self-monitoring that a student can use. Since cognitive flexibility is difficult for students with anxiety as they make a transition from one activity to another, the teacher can work with the student to set up a visual system that pictorially displays each transition during the day. The student is then taught after each transition to record whether they were able to make the transition without becoming upset using self-talk or self-relaxation.

Self-Talk and Self-Relaxation

Self-talk can be another strategy for students who need to monitor their own behavior. It will be important for the teacher to model such behavior. The teacher might say before a class explanation, "I know I can do this." "I have confidence that I can explain this well so that you will understand." Students with anxiety can then be taught to say, "I can stay calm." "I can handle myself in this situation." "I'm scared but I'm going to be okay."

One of the common approaches to reducing stress in both children and adults has been relaxation techniques. Self-relaxation strategies are important for students with anxiety disorders to learn. Students can be taught strategies such as taking deep breaths, closing their eyes and thinking of something that makes them happy, and relaxing their tensed muscles. There are many pieces of music that are designed to calm students that also can be used. Doodling is another method of self-relaxation.

Mindfulness

Researchers are now conducting studies of the effectiveness of mindfulness training for the relief of stress in children and young adults. Mindfulness describes a comprehensive framework that consist of four components—attention regulation, body awareness, emotional regulation, and change in perspective to the self (Martinez & Zhao, 2018). Renshaw and Cook (2017) describe mindfulness as being in touch with what is happening to you in that moment and recognizing unhelpful feelings and changing them. Mindfulness is an "active behavioral process" (Renshaw & Cook, 2017, p. 5). As previously stated in this book, children and adolescents with anxiety have difficulty in these areas; thus, the investigation of mindfulness is an effective strategy for these students. If students are not able to self-monitor and redirect their own behavior, they can face removal from the classroom and the opportunity to learn. Guided mindfulness training can provide that redirection (Martinez & Zhao, 2018).

There are a number of packaged programs available for mindfulness training, some of which have been found effective for the prevention of a relapse of depression and some that have been found effective for students with behavioral problems (Arden, 2016). Meta-analyses have shown that mindfulness strategies are effective at reducing anxiety and depression in adults. For children, initial studies have shown positive results.

Excellent programs, such as *Positive Behavioral Interventions and Supports* (PBIS) (2018), funded by the U.S. Department of Special Education Programs and the Office of Elementary and Secondary Education, involve the prevention of school-wide and classroom-wide problem behaviors. It also provides individualized interventions for students who do not respond to school or classroom programs.

Other programs such as social emotional programs focus on the acknowledgment and management of emotions through skills that develop healthy relationships and bolster motivation. As described by Semple, Droutman, and Reid (2017), these programs teach skills from the outside, whereas mindfulness approaches focus from the inside of the student to improve self-management of attention and self-awareness.

Academic-Behavior Connection

In Chapter 7 of this book, we described a common function of inappropriate behavior as escape/avoidance from tasks that may be or are perceived by the student to be too difficult. If it appears that such tasks increase a student's exhibited anxiety, it is crucial that teachers investigate carefully the academic tasks they are giving the student.

Academics must be engaging and relevant for students. There are an increasing number of students coming into school systems who are disenfranchised. Many feel alienated from the school, while some have been alienated from family, their community, or adults who they believed cared for them but who failed to provide needed assistance. They then enter classrooms with negative judgments, and this sense of alienation may be exhibited by anxiety, depression, and/or aggression. Instructional activities, in areas outside their preoccupation with these feelings of not being in control, are significant in developing student motivation and interest (Jones, Dohrn, & Dunn, 2004). Students can be given assignments where they believe that they are in control. They can be given two choices and allowed to decide which assignment they prefer to do. They can be given a list of three or four topics about which they can choose to write. This will give them a sense of control.

The needs, strengths, weaknesses, and interests of students must be continually reassessed and academic activities planned accordingly. This is a continual process because students with anxiety may have behaviors that vary from day to day, depending on the stressors that they encounter. Teachers can work to identify and decrease those stressors in classrooms and may choose instructional methods that are a match to students' needs.

Worksheets can become a source of frustration and anxiety for students. Some considerations for investigating them to determine whether these assignments could result in problems are as follows:

◆ Does the worksheet have too many questions or problems on it? If it does, divide it up and only give the student one or two parts at a time.

◆ Does the worksheet have multiple sets of directions on one sheet? Remember that students with anxiety exhibit cognitive inflexibility and may have difficulty switching directions.

◆ Does the worksheet have small print? Some students with anxiety may be overwhelmed by small print, and enlarging the print may make it easier for such students.

More accommodations for worksheets will be provided in the next chapter.

Classroom Accommodations

Curriculum and instruction should be filled with hope for students. When children are able to help others they see themselves as valuable to others and see that others need them—a powerful message for students. Their attentions are diverted to helping others rather than only focusing on themselves. Johns (2003) outlines the following steps that teachers can take to incorporate hope in the curriculum.

- ◆ Use a language of hope that includes exposing students to music, visual art, literary art, and performance art that communicates hope and positive messages.

- ◆ Use positive materials, such as those that portray individuals in a positive light and stories with happy endings.

- ◆ Capitalize on the interests and strengths of the student.

- ◆ Provide students with the opportunity to help others through peer tutoring and community service.

Self-Expression through the Arts

Educators are not art therapists. Throughout these chapters, we have provided strategies that are within an educator's scope of practice; however, many students with anxiety disorders have needs outside this scope; therefore, collaboration with other trained professionals who can provide more complex interventions is critical.

For children with selective mutism, it has been noted that while behavior therapies target surface-level behaviors, they do not delve deeper into understanding the child's inner thoughts. Structured play, drama, and the arts have been utilized for students with selective mutism and have been shown to decrease anxiety in all students (Fernandez, Serrano, & Tongson, 2014). The arts provide the opportunity for students to express their inner thoughts in a manner that is non-threatening. Educators can provide excellent experiences that give students the opportunity to express emotions.

The creative arts have also shown promise for students who have experienced complex trauma; this approach is based on the assumption that the verbal part of the brain shuts down during traumatic experience(s) (Panlilo, Hlavek & Ferrara, 2018). Integration of creative forms of expression may allow children to express implicit memories in a non-verbal manner (Dauber, Lotsos, & Pulido, 2015). The arts should be considered a beneficial opportunity for students with anxiety to express themselves, whether it is through the visual arts, music, or drama.

Structured play can serve as the entry point into creative expression (Lusebrink, 2010).

Through the arts, a student can submerge himself in his or her creative potential. Some children cannot face their fears in the real world but through the arts can take risks and explore.

For students who experience anxiety the creative arts can provide a safe space to identify and express feelings.

Activities such as board games, puppetry, and role-playing allow children to process diverse information without the pressure the student may face when completing assignments. A child, who may not want to talk otherwise, may be more likely to engage in a conversation when playing a game.

Throughout this book, readers have been provided with a plethora of creative connections to utilize within the classroom. Music, art, and drama can be incorporated throughout the school day. In math, students can draw pictures of content when completing math problems (add the numbers to learn how many bananas there are, then draw the bananas), learn math songs, and write poetry about math. In reading or literature, students can and should draw pictures and act out the content of stories being read. In social studies, students can cook the food of a country they are studying, draw pictures, and study the arts. The list goes on. The important thing to remember is to incorporate the arts everywhere. This will reduce anxiety, promote creativity, and teach the teacher more about how a student learns best.

Physical Exercise

There is an association between physical activity and mental health in children and adolescents. Sedentary behavior is associated with anxiety disorder. In a large European study of over 11,000 adolescents by McMahon et al. (2017), it was found that girls were more likely to be inactive than boys. According to World Health Organization guidelines, 10.7% of girls were active, and 17.9% of boys were active. The findings showed that even minor increments in physical activity may have substantial benefits to mental health.

A study between physical activity and mental health was conducted with Ghanaian adolescents in 2015 (Asare & Danquah, 2015). The results of this study found that physical activity was significantly associated with good mental health among adolescents. Physical activity was associated with low depression and higher self-esteem.

Studies within the United States have found that sedentary behavior is a risk factor for internalizing disorders in children and adolescents (Gosmann et al., 2015). Children and adolescents are at increased risk for depressive and anxiety symptoms. Individuals with anxiety disorders may avoid group interactions, resulting in less physical activities. Anxiety sensitivity includes a temperament that is characterized by catastrophic interpretations of body physical sensations. Of concern is the association between anxiety and depressive symptoms and cardiovascular disorders. Physical fitness is considered one of the most important health markers, and childhood and adolescence are crucial periods of time to develop a lifestyle of healthy living and activity. Fitness impacts the enhancement of body image which is critical for individuals with anxiety, and it has a direct effect on neurochemicals in the brain such as serotonin or endorphins that elevate mood (Ortega, Ruiz, Castillo, & Sjostrom, 2008).

During the day, teachers can give movement breaks to students by having them do a specific exercise or two. Throughout the day, teachers should encourage movement activities within academics. Here are some examples:

♦ Students can do stretches to answer yes/no questions asked of the group. They can stretch to the left if the answer is "yes," stretch to the right if the answer is "no." Or they can stand up if the answer is "yes," stay seated if the answer is "no."

♦ Carousel brainstorming (musical answers) can be utilized where students move from one station to the next answering questions. Students may have read selected passages in a book or a short story.

The teacher can then post different questions on sheets around the room, assigning a student or small group of students to each question. The student or students write their answer to the question, explaining how they arrived at the answer and any opinions they may have. After most are finished, the teacher plays music which alerts the students to move clockwise to the next station to add their answer at that station. Answers, explanations, and opinions may (and should) differ. This continues until all students have answered all questions.

- Traveling assignments where questions are posted around the room and students move around at their own pace answering the questions are another opportunity for movement.

- Human timelines can be used in history where students line up in the order that the various events occurred. Students can also rate the most important point to them and line up according to those points.

- Four corners can be used for multiple-choice questions. Students are to move to one corner if the answer is A, another corner if the answer is B, and so forth.

- Scavenger hunts for solving a mystery also involve movement. The teacher can hide clues around the room, and students move around the room, trying to find all clues to solve the mystery that may be a specific vocabulary word or a key concept.

TEN TEACHING TIPS

1. Incorporate opportunities for students to help others and to become engaged in activities that result in them witnessing their value to themselves and to others.
2. Provide opportunities for students to be in control of their own destiny through the provision of choices throughout the day.

3. Build a curriculum of hope for your students.
4. Capitalize on students' strengths and interests by incorporating them into curriculum and instruction.
5. Teach students mindfulness strategies such as deep breathing, focusing on the moment, and concentrating on their own body.
6. Teach academics through real-life experiences and through the arts.
7. Proceed with caution when using certain types of worksheets that may result in student frustration.
8. Encourage students to self-monitor their own behaviors through the establishment of personal goals and recording progress.
9. Praise students when you see them regulating their emotions and making transitions effectively.
10. Build movement breaks and academic movement activities throughout the day.

Creative Connections

Choosing My Own Adventure

Students with anxiety often feel powerless in some situations. This creative activity allows the student to think creatively and provide choices on how they want their story to end. This creative connection can be tailored to age, ability, and interests of all students.

Ask the students to write or tell a story about an adventure containing a main character, a setting, and a plot but without an ending. The characters can be animals, people (including themselves if they wish), or superheroes. Have the students share the setting, characters, and plot with a partner or a small group. Students will listen to each other's stories and brainstorm possible changes to the characters, setting, or plot and suggest endings to the story. Each student has the option of using one of the ideas their peers offered or coming up with their own completed adventure. The final story should be written, drawn like a comic, or recorded.

Tessellations

What are tessellations? They are shapes that fit together perfectly, much like a jigsaw puzzle, except the same shape is repeated to create an overall design with no gaps or overlaps. The word "tessellation" comes from the Latin word *Tessera*, which means a small square stone. Tesserae were used in Roman buildings and cathedrals to create mosaics. Tessellations can be simple or complex and address a variety of academic standards in math, geometry, art, and science. They can be adapted for any age class. Students can learn about M. C. Escher, a Dutch artist (1898–1972) who is best known for his mathematically inspired drawings and prints which displayed great realism while at the same time showing impossible perspective, eye trickery, and metamorphosis. Encourage students to find tessellations in everyday life, like in tile floors.

Tessellations can be good for children who exhibit anxiety because it requires focus and repetition. Focusing on one creative task helps students to block out other stressful thoughts. In addition, tessellations look more complicated than they actually are, so students gain a sense of pride in a tessellation's completion. This creative activity can be modified for students of all ages.

For younger grades or students with special needs, create a tessellation, and have students assemble it like a puzzle. Make sure all pieces fit together perfectly with no gaps, no spaces between, and no pieces that overlap. Older students can create their own tessellations. The designs will be an abstract design, but many students enjoy drawing lines to embellish and transform the shapes into animals, faces, or other objects. Very young children and students with special needs may benefit from commercially made tessellation puzzles and games, as well as coloring sheets.

Materials

3" × 5" notecards, 12" × 14" or larger sheets of paper, pencils, scissors, tape, age-appropriate coloring materials such as crayons, colored pencils, markers, or paint.

Directions

Knowing exactly what to do can prevent anxiety. Create visual instructions for drawing tessellations that demonstrate each step of the process. Visual instructions can be at students' tables, posted on the board, or printed for each student. The teacher then gives the following directions:

1. Write your name on the lined side of the card. Turn the card over and hold it horizontally (sideways) in front of you on the table.
2. Draw a line starting from the top left corner (the point where the top and left side meet) toward the middle of the card and ending off the card about a finger's width from the top right corner (on the same top edge of the card). The line can be curvy or zigzag, but remember, you will have to carefully cut on this line, so don't make it loopy or too elaborate.
3. Draw a second line, starting at the top right-hand side and going inward and down to the bottom right-hand corner, and ending off the card about a finger's width from the corner. You should now have drawn a line using the top (long) edge of the card and a second line using the side (short) edge of the card.
4. Carefully cut along the first line. Slide this new little piece downward across the card and line it up to the bottom edge of the card so that the corner where your line started meets the corner directly below it. Carefully tape this piece onto your card.
5. Carefully cut on the second line. Slide this new little piece across the card (sideways) and line up the corner where you started the line with the corner directly across from it. Carefully tape the piece in place.
6. This is a template. You will use this template to make your tessellation design.
7. Drop your template onto your big sheet of paper and carefully trace around all of the sides of the template. It doesn't matter where your template lands the first time. This is your starting point.
8. Slide your template so that it fits like a jigsaw puzzle and trace it again.
9. Repeat step 8 until the page is full. Some pieces will be off the edge of the paper, and that is OK.
10. You should see a pattern emerging. There should be no spaces between each time you trace your template.

11. As you look at your design, do you see shapes and images emerge that resemble faces, animals, or objects? Use your imagination to add lines or marks to embellish this repetitive design. In tessellations, these marks are usually repeated for each shape, but it is not required. You may want to refrain from adding lines and just color in the designs.
12. This is a translation tessellation. Advanced students can explore specific color schemes or other types of tessellations, such as rotational and reflection tessellations.

KEY TAKEAWAYS

♦ Self-monitoring is an important process to utilize with students who are experiencing anxiety because students can see their own progress. It can teach students emotional regulation and cognitive flexibility.

♦ Mindfulness approaches focus within the student, whereas other behavior management systems may focus outside the student.

♦ Relevant, meaningful, and non-threatening academics play a key role in supporting students with anxiety.

♦ Use of the arts in the curriculum can reduce anxiety.

♦ Use of physical exercise throughout the school day promotes positive mental health.

REFERENCES

Abasi, I., Dolatshahi, B., Farazmand, S., Pourshahbaz, A., & Tamanaeefar, S. (2018). Emotional regulation in generalized anxiety and social anxiety: Examining the distinct and shared use of emotional regulation strategies. *Iranian Journal of Psychiatry, 13(3)*, 161–168.

Arden, C. (2016). How does mindfulness training change the narratives of young people identified as having behavioural difficulties? An exploratory study. *Educational Psychology in Practice, 32(4)*, 374–394.

Asare, M., & Danquah, S. (2015). The relationship between physical activity, sedentary behavior and mental health in Ghanaian adolescents. *Child and Adolescent Psychiatry and Mental Health, 9(11)*, 1–8.

Dauber, S., Lotsos, K., & Pulido, M. (2015). Treatment of complex trauma on the front lines: A preliminary look at child outcomes in an agency sample. *Child and Adolescent Social Work Journal, 32*, 529–543.

Fernandez, K., Serrano, C., & Tongson, M. (2014). An intervention in treating selective mutism using the expressive therapies continuum framework. *Journal of Creativity in Mental Health, 9*, 19–32.

Gosmann, N., Salum, G., Schuch, F., Silveira, P., Bosa, V., Goldani, M., & Manfro, G. (2015). Association between internalizing disorders and day-to-day activities of low energetic expenditure. *Child Psychiatry and Human Development, 46*, 67–74.

Greene, R., & Ollendick, T. (1991). Evaluation of a multidimensional program for sixth-graders in transition from elementary to middle school. *Journal of Community Psychology, 21*, 162–176.

Johns, B. (2003). *Effective curriculum for students with emotional and behavioral disorders*. Denver, CO: Love.

Jones, V., Dohrn, E., & Dunn, C. (2004). *Creating effective programs for students with emotional and behavior disorders*. Boston, MA: Pearson.

Lusebrink, V. (2010). Assessment and therapeutic application of the expressive therapies continuum: Implications for brain structures and functions. *Art Therapy: Journal of the American Art Therapy Association, 27*, 168–177.

Martinez, T., & Zhao, Y. (2018). The impact of mindfulness training on middle grades students' office discipline referrals. *Research in Middle Level Education, 41(3)*, 1–8.

McMahon, E., Corcoran, P., O'Regan, G., Keeley, H., Cannon, M., Carli, V., Wasserman, C., Hadlacky, G., Sarchiapone, M., Apter, A., Balazs, J., Balint, M., Bobes, J., Brunner, R., Cozman, D., Haring, C., Iosue, M., Kaess, M., Kahn, J., Nemes, B.,

Podlogar, T., Postuvan, V., Saiz, P., Sisask, M., Tubiana, A., Varnik, P., Hoven, C., & Wasserman, D. (2017). Physical activity in European adolescents and associations with anxiety, depression and well-being. *European Child and Adolescent Psychiatry, 26*, 111–122.

Muris, P. (2002). Relationships between self-efficacy and symptoms of anxiety disorders and depression in a normal adolescent sample. *Personality and Individual Differences, 32*, 337–348.

Niditch, L., & Varela, R. (2012). Perceptions of parenting, emotional self-efficacy, and anxiety in youth: Test of a mediational model. *Child Youth Care Forum, 41*, 21–35.

Ortega, F., Ruiz, J., Castillo, M., & Sjostrom, M. (2008). Physical fitness in childhood and adolescence: A powerful marker of health. *International Journal of Obesity, 32*, 1–11.

Panlilo. C., Hlavek, E., & Ferrara, A. (2018). Neurobiological impact of trauma. In A. Hunter, D. Heise, & B. Johns (Eds.). *Art for children experiencing psychological trauma: A guide for art educators and school-based professionals* (pp. 104–113). New York, NY and London: Routledge.

Positive Behavioral Interventions and Supports. (2018). Retrieved on December 1, 2018, from www.pbis.org.

Renshaw, T., & Cook, C. (2017). Introduction to the special issue: Mindfulness in the schools—Historical roots, current status, and future directions. *Psychology in the Schools, 54(1)*, 5–12.

Semple, R., Droutman, V., & Reid, B. (2017). Mindfulness goes to school: Things learned (so far) from research and real-world experiences. *Psychology in the Schools, 54(1)*, 29–52.

10

Classroom Accommodations

There is no one thing that works all the time.

Eighth-Grade Student

LIVE FROM THE CLASSROOM

Ms. Natalie, a high school teacher of students with special needs, was preparing her students for statewide assessment testing. Corey was diagnosed with high-functioning autism; he becomes nervous in social situations and exhibits test anxiety. When Corey's individualized education program (IEP) conference (Individuals with Disabilities Education Act, 2004) was held, it was decided that he needed extended timelines because of his anxiety.

Ms. Natalie thought she had prepared him for the test. She had taught test-taking strategies, positive self-talk, vocabulary, and more. By state rule, students needing specific accommodations are tested in a separate room. Starting two weeks prior to the test, Ms. Natalie had taken Corey to the testing room for 20 minutes each day and had him do fun activities; this way Corey could meet with success and associate the room with successful experiences. She thought she had prepared Corey.

On the day of the test, Ms. Natalie was responsible for monitoring Corey and three other students not from her class. What she had failed to realize was that there would be other students in that room who also required extended timelines but not necessarily the same amount of extended time.

Ms. Natalie distributed the tests, read the required information to the students, and gave the students the test to do independently. One of the other students, Samantha, whizzed through the test, appearing to just mark any answer, and finished within 45 minutes. She turned in her test and left. Corey saw her and panicked. She was done early, and he was not even close to being done. He began to shake and sweat profusely. Ms. Natalie tried to calm him, careful not to embarrass him in front of the other students who were still working. Twenty minutes later, the other students were finished and left. Corey started crying. Ms. Natalie tried to console him, encouraging him to keep on working. He finally finished the test.

Ms. Natalie was at a disadvantage because she did not realize that there would be other students in the testing room and so had not completely prepared Corey. She realized students with a high degree of anxiety should not be in a room with other students who might finish earlier. When Corey's next IEP came around, she was better able to communicate Corey's needs and recommended that he be tested in a separate room with no other students in the future.

Academic and testing tasks can provoke anxiety in students who become easily frustrated and worried. One can easily imagine that the early finishers knew more and did better. For students with anxiety disorders (ADs), these feelings are amplified.

Involve students in their accommodation plan. Students benefit when accommodations are explained in advance. Out of frustration, they may become agitated and aggressive if they believe that they are no longer in control and do not understand why the teacher may be making these accommodations (Jones, Dohrn, & Dunn, 2004). Children need to perceive that they have control over events. External locus of control, where the student does not believe he or she is in control of a situation, and low self-efficacy are strongly associated with anxiety (Niditch & Varela, 2012).

Before teachers implement accommodations, the student needs to understand the accommodation. Has the student with an extended timeline been taught to manage this time? If a calculator is allowed, does the student know how to use a calculator?

This chapter provides a variety of suggested accommodations for students with anxiety. Accommodations are different from modifications. Accommodations do not change the content of the task or test. They simply provide the tools a student needs to show that he or she knows the topic. Modifications change content. There may be instances where modifications of what is taught must be made.

Accommodations for Attentional Bias

Attentional control is characteristic of students with ADs, particularly generalized ADs and social ADs (Abasi, Dolatshahi, Farazmand, Pourshahbaz, & Tamanaeefar, 2018).

Anxiety can interfere with a student's ability to focus and pay attention. Children who live with chronic stress have an attentional bias toward survival. They have difficulty with activities that require them to think sequentially and concentrate on specific content conveyed. The suppression of distraction involves the ability to stay focused on the desired materials and ignore or suppress the urge to pay attention to irrelevant material. Such distraction suppression is achieved by children who have prior experience with a similar task. They also have good scanning skills (Craig, 2016).

Lectures may be problematic for students because teachers may expect the student to attend to a talk longer than the student is capable. Lectures should be limited to short amounts of time. The teacher may want to stop every five to seven minutes and have students compare notes. This can reduce anxiety for students who are worried that they did not get all of the key points of the lecture. A clear cue such as "This is an important point" tells the student what is important and what should be written down (Johns, 2011).

Advance preparation prior to a lecture can reduce anxiety. The teacher might give the students the notes about the lecture in advance, provide the students with a graphic organizer or an outline of what will be discussed in the lecture, or provide the "big ideas" to the students. Another method is to give the students a lecture guide with the main points of the lecture in a fill-in-the blank format. This encourages the student to pay attention to the lecture while accessing the main ideas. Because these students have difficulty with attention, the teacher should provide as many preparation activities as possible.

When a teacher is giving directions, the teacher should give one instruction at a time, give the direction as a command, and make sure certain students are paying attention when the direction is given. The teacher gives the students praise for following the direction (Kauffman & Badar, 2018). It may be helpful to give one instruction and have the student repeat it.

Accommodations for Memory

Students with ADs may have memory problems. Their anxiety may result in inability to attend to a task or remember the main points. Maehler and Schuchardt (2009) have divided working memory into three components: the supervisory system, the phonological loop, and the visual-spatial area. The supervisory system serves to control and regulate the occurring cognitive processes. In the supervisory area, the student has to retrieve material from long-term memory and determine when to pay attention to the task. In the phonological loop, the student has to process the information that is stored which they may do through a sub-vocal rehearsal. In the visual-spatial process, the student is focused on remembering and processing the visual and spatial information. To perform these components is very complex for students with anxiety because at any point, their attention may not be on the working memory but instead on what is worrying them.

What does this mean for accommodations for memory? It is important that a teacher have a student's attention before focusing on information. This may be accomplished by providing verbal or visual cues to assist the student in retrieving information.

By focusing on a student's interest in a given area, the student will be more likely to pay attention. Music, hands-on activities, or dramatic performances of the information may assist the student in remembering the information.

Mnemonics can be a helpful tool for students. Pictures, associations, and acronyms are valuable. One mnemonic to remember the great lakes is HOMES—Huron, Ontario, Michigan, Erie, and Superior. Teachers and students can also create what is meaningful for them (Steele, 2007).

Accommodations for Language

Children who have experienced trauma resulting in anxiety may have difficulty with spontaneous speech and limited ability to communicate. They have difficulty in spontaneous conversation and may misinterpret body language and facial cues. They may attribute negative intent to innocent feedback from others (Craig, 2016). Giving students visual cues to assist them in expressing might include practice in reading facial cues using videos and magazine pictures.

For students with receptive language problems, use familiar vocabulary when giving directions and assignments. With the generational gap, there may be words a teacher uses that students do not understand.

Necessary vocabulary for the assignments should be taught prior to the lesson. While some textbooks start the chapter with new vocabulary words, a pre-analysis of content may reveal additional words that the students may not understand.

Some students may need help with expressive language skills. Expressive language ability is necessary to answer questions when called upon. Practicing the use of words that express thoughts and feelings is beneficial. Care should be taken not to embarrass the student in front of others. Choices can be given when students are required to engage in classroom presentations, such as preparing a short video that they can edit and then present to the class rather than having them present a live performance.

Accommodations for Cognitive Inflexibility

Cognitive inflexibility is the lack of skills to move from one activity to another without becoming upset and refusing to do so. To cope with transitions that require flexibility, children have to overcome the anxiety, gain information about the new setting, break old habits, create new coping styles, and learn new behaviors (Greene & Ollendick, 1993).

Children who have experienced trauma resulting in anxiety may have difficulty in changing the way they think about something. Perseveration of the past limits their ability to move forward. These children may be stuck in the past (Craig, 2016).

To accommodate a student who has difficulty moving from one activity or subject area to another, the teacher can use precise verbal language to facilitate transitions: "We have three minutes until our next activity," or "Math will be over in five minutes." Visual cues can be effective; teachers may hold up a card with a five-minute warning or ring a bell signaling a transition. However, some students may become hyper-attentive in anticipation of the prompt, being so fearful that they will miss the prompt that they cannot focus on their assignment. For these students, the most effective means of signaling a transition is to announce the remaining time in a calm, quiet voice.

Accommodations for Task Completion

Analyze the Specific Task. Avoid Worksheet Wars

In a functional behavioral assessment of a student with anxiety, the student refused to do makeup work. In the explanation of the behavior, the educator said, "I know he can do the work." When asked how she knew this, she could not answer.

Teachers may erroneously assume that students can do certain tasks. Power struggles and worksheet wars can arise when teachers do not analyze the necessary skills or appearance of the assignment. In looking at a student's unfinished work, pictures were found that blocked text, causing frustration. Sometimes, the visual image of a worksheet can be improved by providing ample white space between content, thus increasing the readability and focus.

On another assignment, the student was expected to switch directions six times on one sheet of paper. The student could not switch gears. Ask the following questions when creating a worksheet:

1. Are there distractions on the sheet that may bother the student?
2. Is the print large enough and clear enough for the student?
3. Is there enough white space on the sheet?
4. Are there too many problems or questions on one sheet?
5. Does the student understand the meaning of the instructional words?
6. Is only one set of directions used on one sheet of paper?

Request that the Student Start the Task

This accommodation is called "Jump Start." Students are more likely to do an assignment if the educator requests that the student start a task rather than telling the student to get the work done. This is less stressful and prevents them becoming overwhelmed before ever getting started.

Premack Principle

This is also known as "Grandma's Law"—first eat your peas, then you get dessert. The student is requested to do a non-preferred task and then the student gets to do the preferred task. This is a strategy that is commonly used with children with autism spectrum disorders—first you do this, and then you get to do that (Johns, 2015). This can also be an effective strategy for children with anxiety because the non-preferred tasks can be broken down into small parts. Once the non-preferred task is completed, the student can engage in a short activity that the student likes to do, such as, "If you do five math problems, you can have five minutes of computer time." When utilizing the Premack principle, it is important that the educator know what students like to do, otherwise the strategy is ineffective.

Fading

The process of fading provides maximum cues to students at the beginning and then slowly and systematically removes those cues. This can reduce anxiety for students because it is a form of errorless learning where students are set up for success. An educator working with a visual learner to read specific words provides a picture representing the word, writes the word, and then color-codes the picture and the word. Systematically, the coloring of the picture fades away; then the picture fades away; and then the color of the print of the word fades away, leaving the printed word.

Accommodations for Perfectionism

Children who exhibit obsessive-compulsive behaviors do not intend to irritate others. They cannot control the behaviors. They may appear to be deliberately stalling to avoid doing an assignment, but they may actually be struggling because they fear they may not get the assignment done perfectly. They may erase mistakes and keep erasing until they have a hole in their paper and then become very upset. Just telling them that their paper is okay is not enough. They are bothered by the fact they had to erase. The educator may decide to break tasks down into smaller steps and provide additional time for assignments and tests (Zimmerman, 2001).

Sometimes a student is so pleased with their progress yet becomes stressed by their perfectionism that they will not complete the assignment. The teacher can encourage the student to breathe deeply and slowly, discuss the assignment, and apply best-case and worst-case scenarios to help the student move forward. A rubric can clearly communicate expectations.

Behavior Momentum

For children with obsessive-compulsive disorder, behavior momentum can be an effective strategy. This involves the utilization of two to four high-probability easy tasks for the student to do before giving them a more difficult task (Johns, 2015). The teacher gives the student an easy task, the student completes it, and the teacher praises. The teacher then gives the student another easy task, and the student is reinforced. This can continue until the student is given a more difficult task, and the student is more likely to complete it.

Backward Chaining

Backward chaining is a process where the teacher does all of the steps except the last one. The student then completes the last step, and the teacher provides praise. The student then completes the last two steps, and the teacher praises the student. The process continues until the student has completed the assignment.

Proofreading Checklists

Providing tools such as proofreading checklists helps students focus on what is expected for a completed task (Johns, 2016). The proofreading checklist can be something as simple as:

Proofreading Checklist

Proofreading Instructions: Use this list to check your work before you hand it in. Keep in mind that your first answers to a test question are often right. Unless you are absolutely sure that your answer is wrong, don't change your answers.

Have I put my name on my paper?
Have I read the directions?
Have I answered all the questions?
Have I checked my spelling?
Have I checked my punctuation?

Scoring rubrics clarify expectations. Teachers can explain the criteria they are looking for in an assignment and how many points each of the different criteria are worth.

For students who experience anxiety give them ongoing feedback prior to turning in an assignment. A teacher can give positive verbal or written suggestions on a draft, thus allowing students to revise before the due date. If an assignment has several parts, give the student one part at a time to reduce the worry about the assignment being perfect. This allows you to provide positive feedback at each step along the way.

Accommodations for Oversensitivity within the Environment

Some students are hypersensitive to a wide variety of factors. The physical environment within the classroom should be calm and comfortable and exude a sense of safety for the student. Fluorescent lights, crowded shelves, a high noise level or new noises, ventilation, and more may upset the student (Sarathy, 2009).

Some students with an AD prefer to sit in the back of the room, so they can see what is happening in front of them. They may become anxious and worried about what people are doing behind them.

Classrooms should have specific areas that are designated for calming the students. These are not punitive areas but areas where the students find a sense of comfort. If permitted, there might be a rocker, a bean bag chair, or a comfy rug with pillows on the floor. When possible, teachers may want to use lamps rather than the fluorescent lights.

Accommodations for Problems with Emotional Regulation

The inability to control emotions is characteristic of many students who have ADs. This deals with how an individual controls emotions, whether adaptively or maladaptively (Abasi, Dolatshahi, Farazmand, Pourshahbaz, & Tamanaeefar, 2018).

Private signals and reminders assist students in emotional regulation. Juan is a student diagnosed with social AD in a large seventh-grade math class. There are 40 students in that class, which in itself may cause anxiety for the student.

Juan's teacher noticed his frustration during a lecture if he did not understand a concept being discussed. The teacher worked out a private signal where the student pulled on his ear, and that was her cue that she needed to re-explain the concept to the class. She figured that if she had not explained it well to one student, there were likely other students who needed it explained differently.

The teacher also noticed other signs that Juan was frustrated. She and Juan spoke privately about ways to be successful in class. They created a special signal that will alert him when she sees he is frustrated. If she sees him bordering on having a minor meltdown, she puts a small sticky note on her pencil as she moves around the room. This signals him to use tools such as self-calming skills to prevent inappropriate behavior.

All students' sensory needs should be met prior to the beginning of class. Is the room predictably set up? Consider the senses of sight (such as a welcoming gesture), auditory (soothing music), olfactory (addressing the smells in the environment), touch (a variety of fidgets), and somatosensory (combination of breath and sound). During a lecture, students can be allowed to doodle or choose a fidget to hold.

Once the sensory issues are met, a child can be taught self-regulation skills. Self-regulation is the ability to appropriately handle sensations of distress when needs are not being met. A student-centered environment helps the students to focus and be mentally present. The basics of breathing are an important component of self-regulation. To encourage breathing in and out, suggest smelling a flower followed by blowing out a candle. When the educator sees that a child is getting upset, she can remind them to breathe in to the count of five and exhale to more than five. Positive self-talk is another self-regulating strategy. The child can learn to say to himself, "I can do this, it's going to be okay." Students recognize when they are engaging in negative self-talk, stop, then switch to positive self-talk.

The arts are an important part of sensory integration and self-regulation. Activities such as doodling, drawing a picture, folding origami, journaling, or allowing students to use headphones to listen to calming music can be integrated into the curriculum.

Building relational skills helps students struggling with emotional regulation. It can provide opportunities for students to work with the teacher, with another student, or with the class. A strategy for educators to use is "I do"—where the teacher models what is expected; "we do"—we work together to do a problem; "you do together"—students work together; then "You do"—a student does a problem independently. Through addressing their sensory needs, teaching them to self-regulate, and building relationship skills, the student should be in a learning mode. A teacher can then provide cognitive activities such as teaching them to read, to understand word problems in math, or how to write a paragraph. If the teacher has not addressed sensory needs, self-regulation, and building relational skills, students are not ready to engage in higher level cognitive tasks.

The educator is a role model, setting a positive example for students. Students need to see educators regulate their own emotions.

Accommodations for Behavior

While ADs are internalizing ones, students who have overt problem behaviors known as oppositional defiant disorders (ODD) may also have internalizing behaviors. In preschool children, attention-deficit hyperactivity disorder (ADHD) and ODD comorbidity ranges from 7% to 14%. A common predictor of disruptive behavior disorders and internalizing disorders is a lack of inhibition. ODD in early childhood may put a student more at risk for acquiring an AD. Difficult temperaments have been linked to both anxiety and aggression. The type of aggression in children with AD and ODD may be more physical than verbal (Martin, Granero, Domenech, & Ezpeleta, 2017).

Supportive Proximity Control

A good practice for teachers is to walk around the room, monitoring the students' progress and providing guidance as needed. This allows the teacher to recognize possible frustration in students and allows for intervention strategies. Supportive proximity control is a de-escalation technique whereby the teacher puts herself in close proximity to the student in a non-intimidating way to provide assistance and positive reinforcement, and to prevent a classroom disruption. By standing in close proximity to the student it usually becomes unnecessary for the teacher to raise her voice or verbally reprimand the student.

Students can also be given personal cards that let the teacher know what is going on with them. The cards might say, "I need help," "I need a short break," "I'm not feeling well, I need to talk with someone." This is an effective means of empowering a student to communicate their needs without verbally calling attention to themselves.

Accommodations for Worry

Children sometimes worry about things that adults do not see as important. Let children know that they can talk privately, thus encouraging them to speak more freely. Active listening is a means of acknowledging the student's feelings. Listen with the goal of understanding. Too often, people stop listening because they are already formulating their responses. Pauses may be appropriate to gain more information or to best formulate a response. Do not deny the child's feelings but affirm what the student is worried about. Sometimes, clarifying questions can enhance communication. Prompts such as "Is this what you mean?" and "Are you worried about _____?" are helpful. Instead of solving the problem, offer assistance by asking, "How can I help?"

If the student is worried about an assignment, saying the assignment is easy may not be helpful. It devalues their feelings. Acknowledge the student's thoughts with statements like "I understand you are worried, let's talk more about it."

Some students worry when they get to a difficult problem. They stop doing any of the assignment because of this one problem, perhaps failing a test as a result. A simple accommodation known as "hurdle help" can assist. Moving around the classroom, a teacher notices that a student is stuck and not proceeding with the remainder of the work; the teacher can approach the student and point out what the student has done right on the sheet and then say, "Looks like you are stuck on number five. How about if you skip it for now and go on to number six? I will then come back and we will do number five together."

Accommodations for Physical Complaints

Children with ADs may exhibit a variety of physical symptoms, such as increased heart rate, nausea, profuse sweating, headaches, shaking, or tremors (Sink & Igelman, 2004). The teacher should work closely with the school nurse, the student, and parents to develop a plan for when the student exhibits a physical complaint. Those complaints should be taken seriously. The student may say he has a migraine headache, and the teacher is torn—is the student making this up to get out of class, or does the student really have a headache? Whether the student has one or not, the student is crying out for help and should be taken seriously. Think about what the class is doing that may be causing stress, and change the activity or give the student a short break. Discussing the issue with the school nurse is a way to seek another opinion, before making a decision.

If the educator sees warning signs that the student is becoming upset, there are a variety of preventative behavioral strategies that can be implemented. "Antiseptic bouncing" is a simple strategy that can be used when a teacher notes that a student is exhibiting physical symptoms of distress such as sweating. Removing the student for just a short period of time can make a big difference. She can request that the student go over and sharpen a pencil or run an errand. The student may need more frequent breaks and use of the restroom when requested.

Angelina is a student who has significant allergies that have been well documented on a Section 504 accommodation plan (Rehabilitation Act of 1973). A 504 accommodation plan ensures that a child with a disability identified under the law who is attending an elementary or secondary educational institution receives accommodations that will ensure their academic success and access to the learning environment. Angelina exhibits a generalized AD. The teacher, thinking that she is helping Angelina by cleaning the room, uses some cleaning products. Angelina has an allergic reaction and has to go home. Angelina is fearful of a repeat reaction. The teacher stopped using those cleaning products. To alleviate Angelina's fearful anxiety, the teacher spoke with Angelina and her parents to assure them that it was safe for Angelina to return to class.

A seventh-grader with an AD ended up in the emergency room with an asthma attack. He became stressed when he was unable to complete the four hours of homework assigned for that evening. It was necessary to talk with all of the teachers to get them to coordinate their homework assignments to prevent too heavy a load for students on any one night.

Accommodations for Test Anxiety

Kathleen became so anxious about one of the state assessment tests that she spelled her own name wrong. She knew the material but could not focus on it because of her anxiety. For students who are frightened by the thought of a test, there are several preparation strategies: practice tests, teaching students how to read directions, how to scan a test, how to move on when they do not know one of the answers, and how to review necessary vocabulary. Many students panic when they do not know an answer—they have to learn the skill of skipping a question rather than becoming stuck and not moving further. Students also need to be taught elimination strategies and how to guess wisely and should be taught test-taking strategies (Johns, 2016).

In preparing students to take tests, it can be helpful to teach them positive self-talk strategies. Student can learn to verbalize those strategies, or they can be posted in the classroom. Students can write them down and stick them to their desks.

Accommodations appropriate for students with anxiety during the test can include extended time, breaking the tests down into small parts, frequent breaks, administering the test in a separate area, and/or special lighting. When presenting the test to the student, the print may need to be enlarged, there may need to be more white space, keywords or directions may need to be highlighted, and visual magnification may be needed. When students are responding, they may need a larger space to respond, use of a computer, spell-check, or a calculator (Johns, 2016).

Accommodations for test-taking must be compatible to those that are used for instruction. Accommodations should be practiced during instruction prior to the test. Do not assume that all students are familiar with using a calculator.

Accommodations for Specific Subject Area Anxiety

Many students experience specific subject area anxiety. Some students will say they hate math, they do not like to read, or they are not any good at science. Negative attitudes make learning more frustrating for these students. Accommodations can include positive reinforcement to the student for engaging in those tasks. Pointing out that the student is doing well is helpful and builds confidence in their ability to succeed.

Educators can build on the interests of the student and incorporate a wide variety of activities to entice them. Teach measurements in math by cooking, teach science with hands-on experiments, and choose literature that matches students' interests.

Choices can be an important accommodation for specific subject area anxiety. If a student has 10 problems, the student may be given the choice of completing the odd-numbered problems or the even-numbered problems. The student can be given the choice of where and/or how to work—at a desk or table across the room, on a laptop, or using a pencil or pen. Choices are a way of empowering the student and can result in the student doing an assignment that he might not want to do. It teaches a student with an AD the life-long skill of making choices and being a decision maker. With students experiencing anxiety, offer only two or three choices at one time because too many choices can result in increased anxiety. A variety of choices should be offered to all students to avoid spotlighting an individual.

In creating a Section 504 accommodation plan or the IEP, include the student and parents in determining any accommodations and identifying criteria. Assess these accommodations on an ongoing basis, and continually re-evaluate them to make sure they are effective.

Documentation of Accommodations

Ms. Natalie realized her mistake too late. Wanting others to be aware of this issue, she documented Corey's future accommodation needs in his IEP. Later chapters will address the legal rights of students with disabilities, whether they are in need of a Section 504 accommodation plan or an IEP. Whatever the student is eligible for, it is essential that documentation for the specific accommodations is found in the student's record and is explained. The statement "extended timelines" may not be enough: A more thorough explanation needs to be provided for future planning for the student.

TEN TEACHING TIPS

1. Watch for signs that the student may be getting frustrated with a particular task and accommodate that student with strategies such as hurdle help and antiseptic bouncing.
2. Utilize behavior momentum when you believe that a task will cause frustration or fear of failure in a student.
3. Use visual cues, interests, music, art, drama, and mnemonics to assist students in memory-related tasks.
4. Request that a student start a task rather than requesting they get all of the assignment done.
5. Acknowledge the worries that the student is verbalizing.
6. Addressing sensory needs and self-regulation are the initial steps to building relationships and cognitive skills.
7. Analyze worksheets to assure appropriate level and appearance to avoid triggering anxiety.

8. Analyze specific vocabulary words used within directions and text for student understanding.
9. Allow students to provide drafts of assignments before turning in the final product.
10. Provide rubrics for students clarifying specific expectations.

Creative Connections

The following creative connections are experiences that help students develop flexibility and allow them to break out of any perfectionistic tendencies that could otherwise impede learning. These creative connections also encourage students to accept and embrace imperfections as part of the creative process.

Let's Get Wild and Crazy!

Option 1: Drawing with the Non-Dominant Hand

Materials

Paper, pencils, (or crayons or colored pencils).

Students often have preconceived notions of perfection, which hinder exploration and experimentation. It can sometimes prevent students from even beginning a task. This simple fun exercise brings out the giggles as students use their non-dominant hand to draw a common image, a tree, a house, or other specific object as directed. Students should share their drawings with others to reveal the variety of marks made on their papers. Students might also note that these images cannot be drawn with perfection and therefore have playful expressive lines.

Option 2: Sculpting Sight Unseen.

Materials

Any type or color of clay, playdough, or air-dry clay.

Directions

Distribute a small amount of clay to each student and ask them to stand and use both hands behind their back to sculpt an animal. The teacher can designate a specific animal for all students to sculpt. Students then present their sculpture to the class. This activity results in laughter and joy, and stimulates conversations about the limits people put on themselves to make products that are considered perfect. What determines the perfect product? Who decides? Does it have to look realistic? Does an object's value reside in its realism or the joy in creating it? What will happen if all results do not look alike?

By sculpting behind the back, the pressure of being perfect is off. It allows for a freedom in the learning process. Play is the earliest form of learning. Sometimes by taking the pressure off, more is learned than expected. In other academic subjects ask the question, "Are there times when focusing on being right, on being perfect, suppresses the joy of learning?"

Option 3: Drip and Splatter Paintings

The objective of this creative connection is to give students who experience perfectionism anxiety an opportunity to really break loose and create an abstract painting that has no right or wrong. In the style of Jackson Pollock, an American painter (1912–1956) best known for his drip paintings as part of the abstract expressionist art movement, students will make drip and splatter paintings that have no pre-drawn images. While this is a messy art project, the therapeutic value to the students makes the mess worth the effort. The students will have the opportunity to move freely, to use color freely, and to engage in expressive mark-making without inhibition.

Materials

Aprons or old shirts; disposable plastic drop cloths; paper towels; masking tape; large sheets of craft paper; tempera paint in a variety of colors; containers for water and paints; tools for painting, such as brushes, sponge brushes, sponge paint rollers, toothbrushes, and twigs; cardboard scraps; newspaper, pencils.

Directions

1. Inform the students in advance that they will be doing a very messy art project and to wear or bring old clothes and shoes.

2. Cover the floors with plastic drop cloths and tape down the edges.
3. Cover work areas with newspaper.
4. Place containers of paint and containers of water on each workstation.
5. Distribute a variety of painting tools at each workstation.
6. Give each student an apron. If students are concerned about their footwear, wrap their feet in old rags or plastic bags.
7. Students can work independently or collaboratively in small groups.
8. Give the students large sheets of paper. The paper may be taped to a wall, placed on the floor, or placed on a table. Paint should go only on the paper and not on each other.
9. Demonstrate various methods of using the paint tools to make creative marks. Students may also use their hands to make marks. This is a good time to remind students that there is no right or wrong way to do this project.
10. Demonstrate cleaning the painting tools to keep the paint colors fresh and clean (they will get muddy if cleaning care isn't taken).
11. Remind the students about cleaning up and that a heads-up will be given before it is time to clean up.
12. Tell the students that you hope to see exciting, colorful splatters and drips and say, "On your mark, get set, go have fun!"
13. Spend a few minutes looking at each completed painting as a class. Talk about what you enjoyed the most about making your marks. When the paintings are dried, display them in the hallways for all to see.

KEY TAKEAWAYS

- Involve the student in designing accommodations so that the student better understands what he needs and feels a sense of control.

- Evaluation of the effectiveness of the accommodations is an ongoing process.

- Documentation of accommodations is essential to better understand the needs of the student.

- Teach the student how to utilize accommodations.
- Choose accommodations that set students up for success.

REFERENCES

Abasi, I., Dolatshahi, B., Farazmand, S., Pourshahbaz, A., & Tamanaeefar, S. (2018). Emotional regulation in generalized anxiety and social anxiety: Examining the distinct and shared use of emotion regulation strategies. *Iran Journal of Psychiatry, 13(3)*, 161–168.

Craig, S. (2016). *Trauma-sensitive schools.* New York, NY: Teachers College Press.

Greene, R., & Ollendick, T. (1993). Evaluation of a multidimensional program for sixth-graders in transition from elementary to middle school. *Journal of Community Psychology, 21,* 162–176.

Individuals with Disabilities Education Act. Pub. L. No. 94–142, 20 U.S.C. sec. 1400 et seq.

Johns, B. (2011). *401 practical adaptations for every classroom.* Thousand Oaks, CA: Corwin Press.

Johns, B. (2015). *15 positive behavior strategies to increase academic success.* Thousand Oaks, CA: Corwin Press.

Johns, B. (2016). *Preparing test-resistant students for assessment: A staff training guide* (2nd ed.). Palm Beach Gardens, FL: LRP.

Jones, V., Dohrn, E., & Dunn, C. (2004). *Creating effective programs for students with emotional and behavior disorders.* Boston, MA: Pearson.

Kauffman, J., & Badar, J. (2018). *The scandalous neglect of children's mental health: What schools can do about it.* New York, NY: Routledge.

Maehler, C., & Schuchardt, K. (2009). Working memory functioning in children with learning disabilities: Does intelligence make a difference. *Journal of Intellectual Disability Research, 53(1),* 3–10.

Martin, V., Granero, R., Domenech, J., & Ezpeleta, L. (2017). Factors related to the comorbidity between oppositional defiant disorder and anxiety disorders in preschool children. *Anxiety, Stress, and Coping, 30(2),* 228–242.

Niditch, L. & Varela, R. (2012). Perceptions of parenting, emotional self-efficacy, and anxiety in youth: Test of a mediational model. *Child Youth Care Forum, 41,* 21–35.

Rehabilitation Act of 1973. Pub. L. No. 93–112, 29 U.S.C. sec. 701 et seq.

Sarathy, P. (2009). *Positive behavioral intervention for students with autism: A practical guide to avoiding the legal risks of seclusion and restraint.* Horsham, PA: LRP.

Sink, C., & Igelman, C. (2004). Anxiety disorders. In F. Kline & L. Silver (Eds.), *The educator's guide to mental health issues in the classroom* (pp. 171–191). Baltimore, MD: Brookes.

Steele, M. (2007). Teaching social studies to high school students with learning problems. *The Social Studies,* March/April, 59–63.

Zimmerman, B. (2001). *Why can't they just behave? A guide to managing student behavior disorders.* Horsham, PA: LRP.

11

Collaboration with Other Personnel and Parents

My daughter's anxiety had been worse than ever, keeping her from doing ordinary things like playing at a friend's house. One day another parent bent down, got eye level to my daughter, and had a short quiet private conversation. Later my daughter looked happy and said, "Ms. Terri said she had anxiety too when she was a little girl. Mom she is the only person who understands what I feel."

Parent

LIVE FROM THE CLASSROOM

Ms. Brenda was a special education teacher in a high school setting for students with significant behavioral challenges. Michael had come to her from his local high school because of a diagnosed oppositional defiant disorder (ODD). Later he was also diagnosed with a social anxiety disorder. Michael responded well to a program which provided a high degree of positive reinforcement and taught self-monitoring skills.

Michael's mother was a single parent working two jobs to raise her three children. Ms. Brenda established a positive relationship with Michael's mother, admiring her support of Michael's educational needs, including attending parent-teacher conferences. Ms. Brenda talked to Michael's mother once a week to let her know how Michael was doing and how proud she was of his accomplishments. She also thanked Michael's mother for the support she gave to the school.

Ms. Brenda worked hard to ensure that Michael made a smooth transition back to his high school. Through the individualized education program (IEP) process, Ms. Brenda started Michael's integration slowly with one class, then two, then three, until Michael was back at his home high school full-time. Ms. Brenda worked with the staff there to ensure that his needs were being met.

Within a month of his full-time return to the local high school, Michael started having significant behavioral issues. Ms. Brenda talked with Michael to gain insight into what was happening. She learned that Michael's mother was not happy about him being at the high school and that his mother really liked the positive phone calls and support she received from Ms. Brenda.

Ms. Brenda had underestimated how important positive feedback and caring was for his mother. Focusing on Michael's needs when planning his return to the high school, she had missed the importance of her support to Michael's mother. She worked with the high school staff to improve their support of Michael's mother.

This scenario occurs more often than one thinks—underestimating the power of collaboration with parents or caregivers. Positive recognition is important for both students and caregivers. Parenting is difficult but perhaps more so with a child with special needs. Team effort is required when teaching students who need assistance.

This chapter focuses on educators working with other personnel, agencies, or families of students.

Working in Partnership with School Personnel

School-based services for students experiencing anxiety play an important role in the early detection of psychological problems, referral for community services, and provision of mental health services in the learning environment. A positive climate of professionals working together can increase the likelihood of successful implementation of services that students need (Santiago, Kataoka, Forness, & Miranda, 2014).

The teacher is not alone in reaching a child who experiences anxiety. She has the support and expertise of the school social worker, the psychologist, the guidance counselor, the nurse, and the administrators. Children who experience anxiety need the assistance of others to meet their social, emotional, and medical needs.

Educators and other school personnel do not have all the answers. They can seek assistance from others who bring a different perspective or additional insight to an issue. A single educator may be too close to a situation to see what is happening. More eyes and ears may provide better insight.

For students who have anxiety and are receiving special education services, cooperative climates and less work overload on each team member can lead to more parent involvement. All educators who work together need peer, organizational support, and training (Santiago, Kataoka, Forness, & Miranda, 2014).

Communication is key: Administrators must be informed at all times concerning students with frequent progress reports. As Shepherd (2010) states, "Administrators, especially the school principal, influence the school environment more than any other factor" (p. 211). When teachers and other support personnel fail to communicate with each other, they may lose very valuable insights helpful to the students' progress.

Strategies for Supporting Parents

Understanding the Needs and Challenges of the Family

It is important to understand the challenges that parents face in raising a child who experiences anxiety. The stress can be great: Parents need support and assistance, not criticism.

Divorce rates among couples who have children with disabilities are higher. Parents may lack social support and coping mechanisms (Hourigan & Hammel, 2018). Experiences within the family structure have been found to predict anxiety (Parrigon & Kerns, 2016). One or both of the parents may be experiencing anxiety. There is evidence that there is a biological component to a familial link, and genetics can account for around one-third of the variance in child anxiety (Williams, Kertz, Schrock, & Woodruff-Borden, 2012).

Parents may be overwhelmed. They are inundated by life's problems and responsibilities, including other children, facing financial pressures, and feeling out of control. They may be exhausted and may need a break once in a while, and they could benefit from respite services available in the community. Educators need to recognize these pressures and assist parents (Shepherd, 2010).

Parenting Styles

Parenting behaviors differ. Anxious parents with children with anxiety disorders are more likely to respond with negative behaviors, resulting in the child modeling those negative behaviors. Non-anxious parents responded with more warmth and the children then modeled that behavior. When a student is unable to regulate his emotions and displays negative behavior, the parent may respond with harsh parenting. This is considered a coercive cycle (Williams, Kertz, Schrock, & Woodruff-Borden, 2012).

There is no one parenting style or type of family functioning that causes child anxiety. However, good relational functioning within an adolescent's family can impact a better long-term outcome on anxiety (Jongerden & Bogels, 2015).

In interviews with parents about what coping strategies best worked with their children, Beato, Pereira, and Barros (2017) found that the majority of parents reported using adaptive strategies. These included actions that regulated the child's anxiety, providing emotional support, encouragement of bravery, and task resolution. Less positive strategies were also mentioned, including those encouraging dependence and parental overinvolvement. When parents were observed in their actual interactions with their children experiencing anxiety, they were often overly involved or intrusive in their interventions, or modeled anxious behavior (Beato, Pereira, & Barros, 2017).

Parents with Unrealistic Expectations

Some parents have unrealistic expectations for their child, and, as a result, the child becomes more anxious. When the child does not meet those expectations, the parents see the child as a failure, causing her to believe that she is a failure (Shepherd, 2010).

Parents may spend a lot of time working with a child to help them improve in specific areas believed to be important, not understanding that unrealistic expectations for the child may lower the child's self-esteem. Parents, as well as teachers and administrators, can build self-esteem by praising the student's success and by recognizing that unrealistic demands may harm the child's beliefs about their value. Academic anxiety in children with learning disabilities is an important variable impacting children's self-esteem. Lower self-esteem can impact relationships and behavior (Sati & Vig, 2017).

Parents with Punitive Approaches

There are parents who use a punitive approach, cannot see when the child does well, focus on what is wrong, and punish the child for something that he cannot do. Focusing on what the child does well and diligence with home-school journals can be effective. In a home-school journal, the educator writes to parents describing student goals, student self-evaluations, and ways to make improvements rather than stressing negative events. The educator can model the importance of building on the positive and celebrating the student's successes. The parent, in turn, writes back in the journal about the child's progress at home.

Parents Who Encourage Overdependence

Some parents encourage their children to be overly dependent on them. They may feel that the child needs to depend on them rather than engaging in independent behavior. Especially if the child faces a new situation, they fear the child will become anxious and fail, thus becoming overprotective. Educators need to encourage parents to provide opportunities for their child to be independent; this may be difficult since no parent wants their child to fail.

Sometimes parents may provide too many accommodations, such as staying home with the child instead of going out, allowing the child to stay home when the child is anxious, or encouraging the child to drop out of sports because of anxiety. These accommodations may result in harm, not help (Benito, 2013).

One mother reports the following: Her eight-year-old son played both Little League Baseball and soccer. One day, when they were driving from Little League to soccer, her son, while changing uniforms in the car, asked, "Do I have to play both sports?" "No, of course not," the mother responded, "Which one do you want to quit?" This scenario reveals a child who was self-aware and able to communicate his needs.

Not all children are that self-aware or able to communicate their needs. Eliminating unnecessary stress is equally important as encouraging children to fulfill a commitment, such as participating in a team sport. Being flexible and allowing a child to make choices encourages independence.

A summary of how educators can support parents who exhibit these different behaviors follows:

♦ A parent who is overwhelmed can be encouraged to engage in active listening, to provide positive feedback, and to utilize respite services.

♦ A parent with unrealistic expectations can be encouraged to work collaboratively with the teacher to learn to provide positive feedback to their child, to learn specific tasks that student can and cannot do, and to set realistic goals.

♦ A parent who is punitive can be provided with a home-school journal, giving examples of positive reinforcement, modeling positive feedback, and praising the parent.

♦ A parent who encourages over-dependency can be provided with examples of what the student can do on her own and can be praised when the parent encourages the student to be independent.

Setting Opinions and Beliefs Aside

Educators may become frustrated and criticize families, believing the parents could be doing more. Why don't the parents cooperate more? They may believe that the parents are pushing too hard or not hard enough or that if the parents would just work a little harder with the child, the child would not have a problem.

Rather than adding to their stress, educators can help parents cope with it by giving them as many tools and support as possible.

Regardless of culture, all families belong in a school's community, feeling that they are an integral part of the educational decision-making of their child. Educators should eliminate language barriers and connect culturally through a strength-oriented perspective, by focusing on what is happening in the family that is positive and what the child does well (Kea, 1997).

Active Listening

Active listening involves listening to what someone is saying, to understand what is being said, rather than preparing to reply. Focus on the message that the speaker is attempting to communicate; refrain from judgment to enable insight into their needs.

At times when a teacher does not know what should be said next, engaging in white-space pauses where nothing is said allows the speaker to continue talking and perhaps clarify what is being related. Providing verbal feedback, paraphrasing what the parent said and asking them to verify that communication, is another technique to ascertain what was actually being said. Asking for a moment to think about what has been said is acceptable.

Supportive Communications

Being supportive means to refrain from judgment and to offer assistance to the family. Statements such as the following will communicate a willingness to help, not judge:

> What can I do to help?
> Is there something you would like me to do to assist you?
> Is there someone else you might like to speak with? Can I help make that connection?
> How can we work together to help your child?

Working Together with Other Agencies and Services

Privacy

Some students with anxiety are involved with other agencies such as mental health services or family service agencies. Some children may be on various types of medication prescribed by a physician. Can the teacher or the social worker communicate directly with these agencies or individuals? The answer in most cases is no. The parent or the student, depending on the student's age, will need to either give or get permission for any information from these agencies to be given to a teacher. Groundwork must be laid to ensure, in working with a parent, that their child's right to privacy is maintained. More on laws governing privacy will be covered in the next chapter.

Since some students with anxiety disorders may be on medication, educators need to understand the adverse side effects of specific medications. Teachers are responsible for monitoring any unusual behaviors that may occur with the student and should notify the parents at once of any changes in behavior, such as self-injurious behavior, suicidal ideation, or an increase in agitation. All teachers are mandatory reporters of suspected abuse or neglect to the state agency responsible for children and family services. (By law, every teacher must report any suspected abuse, neglect, or potential harm to any student.)

Linking Parents to Support Groups and Other Resources

Educators may avail themselves of services that are beyond what the school can provide and are available within their community. There are many regional and national organizations that may provide additional resources. Resources are provided in Chapter 14 of this book.

Take care not to push a service that the parent is not ready to receive; rather, provide the parent with possibilities. The team of educators should work together to learn more about the services that may be available.

Individual and group cognitive behavioral therapy and resilience-based cognitive behavior group therapy have been found to be effective (Watson, Rich, Sanchez, O'Brien, & Alvord, 2014). Resilience-based theory focuses on social competence and the ability to successfully adapt from adversity. It is an asset-based approach that focuses on strengthening protective factors rather than a child's deficits (Heise, 2014). Parents and teachers reported progress in children who had been involved in such a program, with parents reporting that problem behaviors and communication had improved (Watson, Rich, Sanchez, O'Brien, & Alvord, 2014).

Some schools provide parent training within the school. They may schedule speakers who discuss the services that are available within the community: behavior management, fostering independence, or understanding different medications. A physician may speak about health challenges that children face, or a school psychologist may speak about what a case study evaluation involves. This is an excellent way to spread the word about important topics. Whether or not parents avail themselves of these workshops, at least the school has made an effort. To encourage parent participation, schools may want to consider providing child care and transportation to and from events.

The process of working with families and outside agencies to assist a child with anxiety requires communication and teamwork. Some schools have support groups for parents who are experiencing challenging times with their child. These groups are often coordinated by the school counselor and may include other parents who have successfully faced a similar situation.

There are agencies that provide respite services to parents that will vary according to the area where the family resides. The school should keep list on file of these services. Admitting that one needs respite is not an indicator of failure on the part of the parent.

TEN TEACHING TIPS

1. Understand the stressors that families face when a child exhibits anxiety; refrain from judging them negatively.
2. A team approach is advisable when working with students with anxiety. Reach out to others such as the social worker, the school psychologist, the guidance counselor, the nurse, and the administrators.
3. Provide encouragement to the parents rather than being critical.
4. Engage in active listening.
5. Explore services that are available for the student and his family that are outside the school.

6. Work with your team to determine what services the school can provide, such as parent training or a support group.
7. Obtain written parent permission if you wish to communicate with an outside agency or a physician who is working with the child.
8. Monitor any changes in a child's behavior if the child is on any type of anxiety medication, and communicate those changes to the parent.
9. In using home-school journals, be cautious in writing to not convey a message that may result in more anxiety for the child or the family. Keep messages positive.
10. Provide positive recognition to the parent for their efforts in helping their child.

Creative Connections

Collaborative Volunteerism

Doing something for others takes the emphasis off oneself and can create feelings of joy and accomplishment. Teachers can guide students to identify needs in the community, such as hunger and food insecurity, school readiness, homelessness, and the needs of students participating in family youth services. Have students make a list of needs. The teacher may contact local agencies to coordinate volunteer efforts. Older students can often make connections themselves. Possible volunteer activities that may be meaningful to students is to assemble food packages at a local food bank; stuff backpacks with school supplies or comfort items for children in the foster care system or children in homeless shelters. Other necessary items can include toiletries, hats, socks, or gloves. Fun items that may bring joy can be included, such as art supplies.

Reaching Out

Thinking beyond themselves is important for students who have experienced anxiety. Extending the boundaries of the classroom creates a connection with local, national, and international communities. Guide students in a dialogue about people who work to keep them safe, such as first responders (i.e., police, fire-men, paramedics, and emergency medical technicians), active service men and women, and veterans.

Materials

Paper (any type, any color, any size); drawing materials, such as crayons, pencils, colored pencils, and markers; and envelopes. Optional additional materials include magazines, stickers, and stamps.

Process

Have students think about the sacrifices made on their behalf. Students may want to share stories of family or friends who serve. Guide students in creating "Thinking of You" or "Thank You" cards. Students can draw pictures and add text. Young students can illustrate and can dictate a message. For very young children, the teacher can print text representing the inside message on paper to give to each child. Each student can then draw a picture on the front of the card and sign their name and age.

An alternative is to have students work collaboratively to create a banner that can be rolled and mailed to a group of heroes.

KEY TAKEAWAYS

♦ Communication and collaboration are effective in working with colleagues who strive to assist children with anxiety.

♦ Compile a list of service agencies and resources for children and families within their community and keep it updated.

♦ Understand the stressors that families have as they parent a student with anxiety.

♦ Engage in active listening and supportive communication when working with families.

♦ Reinforce families for positive actions that they take to assist their children.

REFERENCES

Beato, A., Pereira, A., & Barros, L. (2017). Parenting strategies to deal with children's anxiety: Do parents do what they say they do? *Child Psychiatry and Human Development, 48*, 423–433.

Benito, K. (2013). Family accommodation in pediatric anxiety: Research update. *The Brown University Child and Adolescent Behavior Letter, 29(7)*, 1, 6–7.

Heise, D. (2014). Steeling and resilience in art education. *Art Education, 67(3)*, 26–30.

Hourigan, R., & Hammel, A. (2018). Family perspectives on access to arts education for students with disabilities. In J. Crockett & S. Malley (Eds.), *Handbook of Arts Education and Special Education* (pp. 267–277). New York, NY: Routledge.

Jongerden, L., & Bogels, S. (2015). Parenting, family functioning and anxiety-disordered children: Comparisons to controls, changes after family versus child CBT. *Journal of Child and Family Studies, 24*, 2046–2059.

Kea, C. (1997). Reconnecting with African-American families. *Reaching Today's Youth: The Community Circle of Caring Journal, 2(1)*, 57–61.

Parrigon, K., & Kerns, K. (2016). Family processes in child anxiety: The long-term impact of fathers and mothers. *Journal of Abnormal Child Psychology, 44*, 1253–1266.

Santiago, C., Kataoka, S., Forness, S., & Miranda, J. (2014). Mental health services in special education: An analysis of quality of care. *Children and Schools, 36(3)*, 175–182.

Sati, L., & Vig, D. (2017). Academic anxiety and self-esteem of learning disabled children. *Indian Journal of Health and Wellbeing, 8(9)*, 1024–1026.

Shepherd, T. (2010). *Working with students with emotional and behavioral disorders.* Upper Saddle River, NJ: Merrill.

Watson, C., Rich, B., Sanchez, L., O'Brien, K., & Alvord, M. (2014). Preliminary study of resilience-based group therapy for improving the functioning of anxious children. *Child and Youth Care Forum, 43*, 269–286.

Williams, S., Kertz, S., Schrock, M., & Woodruff-Borden, J. (2012). A sequential analysis of parent-child interactions in anxious and nonanxious families. *Journal of Clinical Child and Adolescent Psychology, 41(1)*, 64–74.

PART III
Ethical and Legal Issues

12

Respecting Students' and Parents' Right to Privacy and Abiding by Confidentiality Laws

I don't have to tell my friends anything. 'Cause they all know. They have seen me cry in class when I can't control my worry. It makes me more anxious trying to think about what they are thinking.

A Fifth-Grade Student

LIVE FROM THE CLASSROOM

Mrs. Marino has a student in her fourth-grade class who is being treated for an anxiety disorder. Mrs. Marino is working closely with her student's parent and the school social worker to meet Jamie's needs. Jamie is on medication and is receiving cognitive behavioral therapy outside of school. Because Mrs. Marino teaches in a small town, it seems that everyone knows everyone's business.

Mrs. Marino's good friend is Jamie's aunt who is also a teacher in the school where Mrs. Marino teaches. The aunt doesn't have

Jamie is her classroom. Jamie's aunt stops by Mrs. Marino's class often after school and asks about Jamie. Mrs. Marino feels free to discuss how Jamie is doing because this is a relative. Mrs. Marino also knows Jamie's therapist who provides cognitive behavioral therapy. They openly discuss how Jamie is doing in school and exchange information. One day, Jamie's mother came to school upset about the information Mrs. Marino had given to the aunt and the therapist. Mrs. Marino explains that she is just trying to keep the lines of communication open.

Communication is important but not appropriate when it involves someone who does not have the need to know the information, like the aunt. Communication is also important with a therapist practicing outside the school; however, it is not appropriate unless the parent has specifically given written permission. What can or cannot teachers share with others?

What Constitutes a Record?

Teachers keep all types of records: a record of grades, notations about students' behaviors, logs, and letters or emails sent to parents. They keep a record of calls to parents and communications with their school administrator, social worker, or psychologist. Personal notes kept by educators may or may not be private.

"A record is anything recorded by hand, digitally, or by audio means that is shared with another individual" (Johns, 2016, p. 103). What exactly does this mean? Teachers may keep logs of student's behavior. If they never share the information with another person in the school or with the parent, then it is a personal note. However, once they share the information contained in the log, it becomes a record.

A teacher attends a meeting with a parent and brings her personal notes so that she can refer to them. The parent asks the teacher for a copy of the notes. The teacher states that these are her personal notes and will make a copy of the information she has shared with the parent. The parent can have the information because it was shared.

When children have anxiety problems, a panic attack, or meltdown due to a change in routine, the teacher may want to keep records of that event. It should be noted that if the teacher documents information, and the information is shared, then the information becomes part of a temporary record.

There are two types of records that are kept about students. The Family Educational Rights and Privacy Act of 1974 (FERPA) is the federal law that governs the types of records and when they can be released, to whom, and how. One record is a permanent file that is maintained without a limitation on time. Such records include basic identifying information about the student which includes name, address, phone number, transcript, and attendance record. Nothing in a permanent record can denote any disability that the student may have. After mandatory notice to the parents that the record is no longer needed to provide education services to the student, temporary records may be destroyed at a parent's request. This record contains evaluations conducted about the student; discipline records or other incident reports; 504 plans under the Rehabilitation Act of 1973, also known as an Individual Accommodation Plan; and individualized education programs (IEP) (Individuals with Disabilities Education Act [IDEA], 2004).

When students receive special education services, educators need to understand IDEA and know what they can and cannot share. Under FERPA, families and students have the right to confidentiality including information in educational records and health-related data (Repetto, Gibson, Lubbers, Gritz, & Reiss, 2008).

The Importance of Accurate Documentation

The information placed in a record must be worded very carefully. It should be based on fact, not opinion. In documenting information, clearly state whether the event was observed or if it was reported to the recorder. For example, "Mrs. Smith came to me and reported that she saw Erika attempt to cut herself while in the cafeteria today at 12:15 p.m." The more details in any report, the better, provided it is accurate and reflective of what happened. Whatever is written and shared with anyone else is part of the student's record and a parent has the right to a copy. Thus, all records should be defendable as to what was written and observed.

All documentation must be signed and dated, and should include the role of the reporter, all efforts to assist the student, and any patterns of behavior that occur. If the educator has spoken with the parent about concerns, this and the parent's response should be documented. Any request for evaluation of students for special education services should be in writing with a copy retained. It is important to keep copies as evidence of efforts to seek assistance for students.

Access to Records

The student, parent, or guardian has a right to review and request a copy of the records. The records' custodian of each school district is responsible for the records, including knowledge of who has records, where those records are located, as well as any school district policy regarding duplication fees for families.

A parent or student requesting records meets with the records' custodian, who explains district policy and prepares copies of the records. Once the student exits the school system and is of the age of majority, some schools notify the family that the records are available to be picked up or they will be destroyed.

Additional information about processing records, what happens if there is a dispute about its content, and what can be destroyed can be found on each state's department of education website. Each school district has policies and procedures regarding disputes as to its contents.

Sharing Information

In deciding who can have access to a child's records, ask whether the individual has the right to know. FERPA allows for the release of information without written parent consent to other individuals within the school system who have a valid educational concern. This means that if the student with anxiety is seen by the classroom teacher, social worker, members of the 504 or IEP teams, or any individual who works with the student has a right to know. Individuals who do not have the right to know, such as the aunt of the student in our opening scenario, should not have access to the information.

Records can be shared when a student moves from one public school to another. When a student moves from a public school to a private or parochial school, records cannot be shared without written permission from the parent/guardian. When agencies, physicians, counselors, or others working with a student request records, the school district must get written permission from the parent/guardian.

There is an exception in FERPA to this rule: If it is deemed there is an issue about the safety of the student or the safety of others, then in an emergency, the educational team could share the information. Records can also be shared with authorized state and federal government officers, and certain judicial and law enforcement agencies (Murdick, Gartin, & Crabtree, 2002).

Understanding the Right to Confidentiality

When educators know specific information about a student who has a special need, such as an anxiety disorder, the student's right to privacy must be respected, including monitoring of the educator's behavior. Violations sometimes occur when educators are oblivious or lack knowledge of the laws and are made because individuals do not realize the serious impact of these statements (Johns & McGrath, 2009). Discussing information about a student with other teachers in the hallways or teachers' lounge is an example of teachers inadvertently breaching confidentiality. These conversations can be overheard and then passed on as gossip.

Some examples of violating a student's confidentiality are announcing to a student in front of the class that his counselor from the mental health agency is here to see him (the teacher is announcing that the student has mental health issues) or reminding a student that he needs to go down to the office to get his medication (the teacher is announcing that this child has health issues). Statements about the mental and physical health needs of students must be said privately (Johns & McGrath, 2009).

At the secondary level, the educator should not ask, "Does anyone in this class need accommodations such as extended timelines?" A student should never be put in this position. A better way to handle this situation would be to announce to the class, "If anyone needs special accommodations, please talk to me privately at another time."

Teaching Students about Respect for Privacy

Students and/or their parents will often share information about their child with other students or other parents. This is the parent's prerogative, and if the student is of the age of majority, that student has the right to share their information. However, without written permission, that parent or student who received the information does not have the right to share it with anyone else.

Confidential health information is defined as "any personally identifiable information about a student's past or present health and development status" (Schwab et al., 2005, p. 11). At the upper elementary and secondary level, educators are cautioned to keep health-care lessons generic and not to address issues specific to one student. Assignments to students that cover student-specific health issues and any grading should not require a student to share personal information (Repetto, Gibson, Lubbers, Gritz, & Reiss, 2008). Teach all students respect for privacy, the importance of confidentiality, and the need to respect the dignity of any individual who may have a special need such as an anxiety disorder.

Parents and educators need to teach students about their disability and how to disclose that information themselves in an appropriate manner. If students have anxiety, they need to learn about accommodations available to them in the classroom. Students have to balance the potential personal cost of revealing health information to others while at the same time revealing the information to people who can assist them (Repetto, Gibson, Lubbers, Gritz, & Reiss, 2008).

People First Language

Teach "People First Language." Adults and students are people first rather than people defined by their disability. This is a lifelong skill that students should be taught. Rather than saying, "She's OCD," or "Betsy is a nervous wreck," it is more respectful to say that "Marie has OCD" or "Betsy has anxiety." Educators should never demean any individual. Making statements such as "Jill, what is your problem today, you are all over the place" demeans a child who has very real anxiety. Saying, "Seems like you're having a tough time today, how can I help?" is a much more appropriate statement.

Treating people with respect is a lifelong skill and should be practiced every day.

TEN TEACHING TIPS

1. Be cognizant that any information that is shared becomes part of the student's temporary record.
2. Only share information with those in the school who have a need to know.
3. Prepare documentation in writing about a student's behavior to determine whether there are patterns.
4. Ensure that all documentation that is subject to parent review is written in an objective manner.
5. Monitor conversations from one student to another student about a third student so that the right to privacy of all students is respected.
6. Teach students about what health information they should or should not share with others.
7. Teach students about the right to privacy and the importance of confidentiality.
8. Model and teach students to use "People First Language."
9. Avoid health-care lessons or assignments that address an individual student-specific issue or require a student to disclose health information.
10. Establish classroom rules about confidentiality.

Creative Connections

Chain of Gossip

Words matter. Sometimes, received information may not necessarily be accurate. When repeated as gossip the sharing of misinformation may hurt someone. This activity helps students realize how easy it can be to misconstrue information.

Procedure

Introduce students to the art of Norman Rockwell. Show them his painting entitled *The Chain of Gossip* and ask, "What is happening in this painting?" "What do you see that tells you that?" "What else can you see?"

The telephone game is a good example of how information can be misconstrued. Have students sit in a circle. Give the first student a message written on a piece of paper that only that first student will see. This message should be a sentence or two (not one word or phrase). Sample sentences: "Mrs. Corcoran was running late for work today and ended up wearing one black and one blue shoe"; "My neighbor, Bill Springsteen, wrote a story that ended up in the paper"; "Linda, a cheerleader at Woodhaven High School, fell while doing a handstand and ended up in the hospital with a broken bone."

Instruct the student to whisper that message to the person sitting to the right of them. Repeat this action until all students in the circle have had the message whispered to them. Ask the last person to reveal the message out loud. Compare the message given to the first student, to the message shared by the last student. While this activity results in laughter, it can stimulate important thoughts about gossip and how information can change or be misconstrued each time it is shared.

To Tell or Not to Tell—Secret Languages
Code Breaker

This creative connection emphasizes the importance of privacy and confidentiality. Children can have anxiety over what to reveal about themselves and what to keep a secret. They can also experience anxiety over what to do with something a friend told them in confidence. Another source of anxiety is being talked about in a negative way by other students. Learning the importance of respect, privacy, and confidentiality can benefit all students.

Procedure

Facilitate a dialog with students about privacy and confidentiality. Sometimes private information is shared among friends.

At first it may seem harmless to share information that you have heard from another. But repeating information can sometimes result in pain or harm to ourselves or others. If a friend shares something that alerts you to the possibility that they are being harmed or will harm themselves or others, it should be shared with an adult—that is not considered gossip. It is not a secret that should be kept.

Ask students about a time when (if) you told someone something in confidence and later found out that the friend blabbed your secret to someone else. Sometimes you can tell your best friend a secret, like the fact that you have a crush on a kid in your class, then your best friend tells the whole world. How does that make you feel? How do you think you would feel if you were the one who told the secret? When is it okay to tell a secret, and when should we not tell it? Secrets can be safe or unsafe. It is important to listen to our instincts and cues, and protect ourselves and others from any potential harm.

Students will create their own secret language and invite peers to try to break their code. Begin by having students write numbers 1 through 26 on a piece of paper. It doesn't matter if this is done vertically or horizontally, the important thing is to have enough space to write a letter next to or under each number. Pick a number on the list and start writing the letters of the alphabet from A to Z. When you get to #26, continue with #1 to complete the alphabet. For example, if a student started with the letter A on number 13, then the letter Z would be number 12. Every student's code will be different. After you have your code, create a secret message using your numbers. Be sure to write your name on the bottom. Exchange with another student and try to decipher each other's secret messages. Secret codes can be used in personal journals. They can be used to communicate private messages with a friend. They can just be used as a fun way to lessen anxiety.

KEY TAKEAWAYS

♦ There are two types of student records. Permanent records will not include any information about a student's special needs and temporary records will.

- FERPA governs how records can be released and to whom they can be released.

- Student records can be requested by the parent and/or the student.

- Students should be taught about the privacy of their own records and the privacy of other students' information.

- Teachers must be very careful in the disclosure of any information about a student and should model the use of "People First Language."

REFERENCES

Family Educational Rights and Privacy Act. (1974). 20 U.S.C. section 1232g; 34 CFR Part 99. Individuals with Disabilities Education Act. (2004). 34 CFR 300.613.

Individualized Education Program. (2004). 20 U.S.C. Section 1414; 34 CFR 300.321 to 300.328.

Johns, B. (2016). *Your classroom guide to special education law.* Baltimore, MD: Brookes.

Johns, B., & McGrath, M. (2009). Be careful what you say: Respecting the privacy rights, equity, and dignity of individuals with special needs. *The Delta Kappa Gamma Bulletin, 75(2),* 20–23, 26.

Murdick, N., Gartin, B., & Crabtree, T. (2002). *Special education law.* Upper Saddle River, NJ: Pearson Education.

Rehabilitation Act. (1973). Section 504 allowing for reasonable accommodations. 29 U.S.C. Section 701 et seq.

Repetto, J., Gibson, R., Lubbers, J., Gritz, S., & Reiss, J. (2008). Practical applications of confidentiality rules to health care transition instruction. *Remedial and Special Education, 29(2),* 118–126.

Schwab, N., Rubin, M., Maire, J., Gelfman, M. H. B., Bergren, M. D., & Mazyck, D. (2005). *Protecting and disclosing student health information: How to develop school district policies and procedure.* Kent, OH: American School Health Association.

13

Legal Protections for Students with Anxiety Disorders

> I had no idea what my legal rights were. Knowing my options and having a team to work with has been life-saving.
>
> A Parent

LIVE FROM THE CLASSROOM

Mr. Saputo has Jennifer in his third-grade class. It is now November, and he is unable to get Jennifer to complete math assignments; instead, she cries. She is reading but only at a late first-grade level. Mr. Saputo calls Jennifer's mother to discuss his concerns. She is also concerned as Jennifer is exhibiting a number of fears and anxieties at home. She is afraid of the dark, wants to follow her mother around, has no friends, and does not go outside to play. Jennifer's parents are divorced, and Jennifer rarely sees her father. When her father comes to take her out, she clings to her mother and will not go.

Mr. Saputo asks Jennifer's mother whether she thinks she should have an evaluation done by the school to determine an appropriate education plan. Jennifer's mother is eager to find out what is happening with Jennifer and is concerned that she might be retained. The teacher last year had suggested retention but then changed her mind. Mr. Saputo assures Jennifer's mother that he will talk with the former teacher and principal and get back to her to see if they agree that an evaluation should be done.

The Right to an Evaluation

School Evaluations

When it is suspected or known that a child has a disability, educators are legally responsible, with written parental permission, to request an evaluation. Parents also have a right to request an evaluation and should be informed of their rights.

Kauffman and Badar (2018) warn against developmental optimism—that is, thinking that the student will outgrow the problem. Evidence is on the side of treatment, but non-treatment is what tends to occur. To receive treatment an evaluation must be made.

In a California legal case, *San Diego Unified School District* (2011), a child at the age of six, receiving services for students with speech problems, began to have behavioral issues. He was having difficulty playing with classmates, and his mother reported that he was beginning to withdraw socially. When the student's case manager assured the parent that the child might outgrow it, the parent did not agree and filed for a due process hearing, a process that occurs when there is a dispute between the parent and school personnel. The hearing officer ruled in favor of the parent, in that the district had sufficient information based on school performance and his mother's report. The district was required to reevaluate the student and address the child's social-emotional needs (Kline, 2017).

Parents must provide written informed consent before a comprehensive evaluation can be completed by school district personnel (Hulett, 2009). School district personnel are responsible for informing parents of the purpose of the evaluation, what the evaluation will consist of, what insight will be gleaned from the evaluation, and answering any questions they may have.

Independent Evaluations

An independent evaluation is one that is conducted by someone, not employed by the school district or other public agency responsible for the education of the child, who is qualified to conduct the evaluation (Kline, 2017). The parent may have sought and paid for an independent evaluation and brought the completed evaluation to the school. The school may have requested an independent evaluation. A third situation occurs when the parent requests an independent evaluation paid for by the school.

Recognition of Parentally Sought Independent Evaluations

If parents have independently had their child evaluated, they may bring that evaluation to the school and ask for accommodations or other services. The district has an obligation to put together the multidisciplinary team to develop an individualized education plan (IEP) to consider the results of the evaluation (IDEA, Regulations). The IEP team does not have to accept or implement the recommendations but they must consider them, providing written documentation about their rationale for not accepting it. They may also wish to conduct their own evaluation to determine how best to meet the needs of the student and to show they are acting in good faith.

Independent Evaluations Requested by the School

Where the school district recommends the child be evaluated by a doctor, the district may be responsible for payment (Murdick, Gartin, & Crabtree, 2007).

It is important to remember that even in the absence of a medical diagnosis the district does not have the right to deny a school evaluation. In a case in South Dakota (*Artichoker v. Todd County School District*, 2016), a parent requested that their seventh-grade daughter with post-traumatic stress disorder be evaluated by the school district. The school district did not do the evaluation. The student was suspended from February through the end of the school year. The district maintained that it needed a medical diagnosis to have knowledge of a disability. The court stated that under the Individuals with Disabilities Education Act of 2004 (IDEA) the district had knowledge that the child had a disability because the parent had requested an evaluation (Slater, 2017).

Independent Evaluation Requests by the Parent to Be Done by the School

If the school district has conducted an evaluation with its own staff, and the parents do not agree with the results, the parents have the right to request an independent evaluation at the public school's expense. The school district has two choices: Pay for an independent evaluation by someone holding the same credentials as the person whose part of the evaluation was disputed, or take the parents to a due process hearing to establish that their evaluation is correct.

Conducting an Evaluation

The Role of the School in the Evaluation Process

When the school suspects or has knowledge that a student has a disability, they are obligated to evaluate the child and cannot place barriers to conducting the evaluation. Schools are required to provide an evaluation that is multidisciplinary, conducted by a team of individuals including the school psychologist, the school social worker, the counselor, the teacher, the school nurse, parents, the student, and others. It should be comprehensive considering health issues, social/emotional issues, cognitive skills, motor skills, and other components deemed necessary. Perhaps a social developmental study is essential when determining the existence of background issues impacting the student's anxiety. The evaluation must be non-biased and thorough.

The team will collect background information, review previous evaluations, and include the parents throughout the process.

After the parents provide written permission, there are specific timelines in each state within which the evaluation must be completed. Evaluations must be conducted every three years for a student who is already receiving special education services.

The team will review the evaluation and make a determination and recommendations. This decision is very serious for the student and warrants comprehensive evaluations.

If the team, through thorough documentation and evaluation, determines that the student does not have a disability, then the process would end. However, even when a disability is not found, it is hoped that a good team will talk about ways they can assist the student's success within the school.

If the team determines that there is a disability, then the next question is whether the disability has an adverse effect on educational performance. If it does not, a plan would be developed under the Rehabilitation Act of 1973 (Section 504). There are students who may have an anxiety disorder but are able to achieve within the classroom and do need accommodations for their anxiety (see also Chapter 10).

If the student's disability shows an adverse impact on their educational performance, the child could need special education services and an IEP would be developed by the team.

A Section 504 accommodation plan differs from an IEP. The differences will be discussed later in this chapter.

Determining Whether the Student Needs a Section 504 Accommodation Plan

A disability as determined by Section 504 is a physical or mental impairment that substantially limits one or more major life activities, which can include but not limited to caring for oneself, performing manual tasks, seeing, hearing, eating, sleeping, walking, standing, lifting, bending, speaking, breathing, learning, reading, concentrating, thinking, communicating, and working (Americans with Disabilities Amendments Act of 2008). It is a very broad definition for who has a disability, and a student who has been diagnosed with an anxiety disorder would be considered as having a disability.

In a California case (*P. P. v. Compton Unified School District*, 2015), students and teachers claimed that exposure to a traumatizing event is a disability and that the school district failed to properly accommodate students. The students and teachers alleged that the district did not meet its obligation to accommodate trauma in the schools and did not train staff to understand the trauma. It was determined that the students and teachers could make a claim based on trauma as a disability. The court ruled that there was a private right of action (Robinson, 2016).

Components of a Section 504 Accommodation Plan

When discussing the creation of a Section 504 plan, there is no requirement for parent agreement, unlike an IEP which does require written parental agreement. A Section 504 plan includes specific services designed to help the students overcome their disabilities, including a list of needed instructional materials, accommodations, grading and assessment changes, and a behavior intervention plan (Sulkowski & Storch, 2012).

A Section 504 plan includes:

1. The evaluation data determining that the student has a disability. A thorough description of the evaluation, particularly as it relates to the needs of the student in the classroom, is beneficial.
2. A summary of the performance of the student in the classroom. Any summary statements about the educational performance of the student should be written in MOO terms: statements that are measurable, observable, and objective. Rather than stating that a student gets worried, one option would be to say that when given an independent math assignment at the fifth-grade level, the student cries half of the time. The educators can measure this, it is observable, and it is objective.
3. The multidisciplinary team, and not just one individual, determines the specific accommodations and who is responsible for implementing them. Accommodations are based on the individual needs of the student and the team must consider the preferences of the student. An accommodation should be designed to help a student, rather than expect a student to do something that he does not like or know how to do.

Implementation of the Plan

Those educators responsible for the implementation of the plan should be listed on the plan. For instance, the student with anxiety may have significant problems in physical education because she is uncomfortable undressing in front of other students. The physical education teacher would be responsible for implementing an accommodation that the student dresses in a separate area or that the student is not required to change clothes for physical education. In another case, the student has an anxiety disorder related to the allergies. The accommodation plan will need to specify what the student's allergies are and what products can or cannot be used within the classroom. If the student is given extra time, does he know how to manage his time?

Protections for Students with Anxiety Disorders under Section 504

Students who have been diagnosed with an anxiety disorder are protected by Section 504 which is an anti-discrimination law. Students with anxiety disorders must be afforded an education comparable to that which all students receive and cannot be discriminated against because of their disability. A school cannot exclude a student with an anxiety disorder from a field trip because of his anxiety problems. If all other students are afforded an opportunity, accommodations should be made to allow the student with anxiety to go on the field trip.

Determining Whether the Student Needs Special Education Services

If the evaluation shows an adverse impact on educational performance, the student may be eligible for special education under one of the 13 categories in the IDEA. Those categories include intellectual disabilities, hearing impairments (including deafness), speech-language impairments, visual impairments (including blindness), serious emotional disturbance, orthopedic impairments, autism, traumatic brain injury, other health impairments, or specific learning disabilities (IDEA Statute, 2004). Some children with anxiety disorders may be eligible for special education under the category of other health impairments or serious emotional disturbance.

There is a category for children aged three to nine who, at the discretion of the state and local district, may be served as children experiencing a developmental delay (IDEA Statute, 2004). When, based on the multidisciplinary evaluation, a team is uncertain about the specific nature of the disability, depending on their state and local district, the team can determine that they will specify a developmental delay until they are able to better ascertain the student's needs (Johns, 2016).

Components of an IEP

A student who is eligible for special education has an IEP. The IEP is a comprehensive document, unique to each student, outlining the student's needs and how they will be met. Completed once a year by the multidisciplinary team, the IEP details present levels of academic achievement and functional performance; strengths of the student; parental concerns; goals and objectives (objectives are required in an IDEA for students with the most significant intellectual disabilities and may be required for other students as determined state by state); specially designed instruction, accommodations, and/or modifications; specific placement; and related services based on the needs of the student. Examples of specially designed instruction for a student with anxiety disorders might be: direct instruction of emotional regulation strategies, teaching the student skills to be cognitively flexible, or positive self-talk strategies. Other special components of the plan might be behavioral interventions or transition plans.

Placement Issues in Special Education

Once the team determines the student's special education needs, they must determine how and where those needs can be met. Teams must provide a free, appropriate public education within the least restrictive environment, meaning the student is educated to the maximum extent appropriate as their peers without disabilities. Schools must have a continuum of alternative placements for students, offering many options ranging from the general education classroom with consultation, to resource services, to instructional classes, to specialized facilities.

Placement cannot occur without the informed written consent of the parent. The team, including the parent, considers options and determines how best to work together to ensure the student's needs are met. Under Section 504, students with anxiety disorders who are in special education are also afforded the rights to an education that is free from discrimination.

The laws described in this chapter are designed to protect the needs of students and to ensure that, in whatever setting, the student is provided a free, appropriate, public education. That education requires an assessment, a review of the assessment, and the accommodations to which the student is entitled. If there is an adverse impact on educational performance, specific special education services to meet the needs of the student with anxiety disorders must be provided.

TEN TEACHING TIPS

1. When it is suspected or known that a child has a disability, a teacher should document the information in writing, keep a copy, and provide that documentation to an administrator or special education coordinator to initiate a multidisciplinary evaluation.
2. Parents should be encouraged to keep a file with all documents related to the child's special education services.
3. The teacher should keep documentation about the student's social-emotional and academic needs because as an important member of the evaluation team and he can share valuable insight.
4. If progress monitoring has been conducted or specific tests given, this information should be shared.
5. Be well prepared for any team meeting for a student, whether it is to review an evaluation to determine whether the student has a disability, write an accommodation plan, or develop an IEP.
6. If a student is eligible for accommodations through a 504 plan because she has a disability which does not have an adverse effect on educational performance, research and be prepared to discuss accommodations that the student will need.
7. When determining accommodations for students, it is important to assess the student's preferences, and teach the student how to use the accommodation.
8. If a student is eligible for special education services, it is important that the teacher come well prepared to present

levels of academic achievement, functional performance, specific needs of the child through goals, and how those goals can be met.

9. When describing the present levels of the student and the goals, remember that all such documentation should be written in MOO terms—Measurable, Observable, and Objective.

10. Monitor the student's progress throughout the process of services to determine the effectiveness of interventions provided.

Creative Connections

Mental Health Advocacy

This creative activity is geared for secondary students but can be modified for younger students.

Introduction

This activity focuses on advocating for students' rights, confidentiality, and respect for mental health. It is beneficial for students to learn about anxiety and other mental health issues, as well as how to be an advocate for themselves and others. This includes knowing educational legal rights and available resources.

Procedure

1. Have students list what they already know about anxiety, mental health, and educational legal rights.

2. Have them list what they want to learn. Guiding prompts to stimulate student thinking and discussion might be: What is mental health? What is anxiety? What are the types of mental health issues that you are concerned about today, such as drug addiction, suicide, and depression? What can we do to advocate for improved mental health?

3. Ask students to research available resources including local, national, and online organizations. Remind students that other people in their community can be valuable resources. Students can interview individuals in their community

about their area of expertise. Local mental health organizations often offer programs and other resources.

4. Create a plan to advocate. The plan should be written in a clear, concise manner, and include a timeline. Make copies available for interested parties. Consider the Why, Who, What, Where, When, and How. What is needed in our school? What resources are available and should be requested? Who should be included? Who is the intended audience? Who are potential committee members and speakers? What resources would be needed, such as speaker honorariums, space reservations, security, advertising? Would a schoolwide program to help students, parents, and teachers be an option?

5. Have students prepare a report to be presented to administrators. Students need to present information gleaned in a professional manner. Make a list of organizations and resources, including potential experts in the field and contact information for available speakers. Students should make an appointment with the principal and/or other school administrators to discuss the information gleaned and their proposals. At the meeting, ask administrators who will handle the logistics of an event (location, time, security, custodians).

6. Once permission is granted, a speaker identified, and a date, time, and location determined, the students develop a specific implementation plan. This plan can be revised as more information is gained. Have students create a chart with specific tasks, responsible persons, and contact information, plus meeting dates, times, and places.

7. The meeting should also include strategies for publicity. Who will issue the invitations to parents? What district persons will contact media outlets, such as television, newspapers, and social media to promote the event. Students can make posters and design flyers to be distributed around the school and community. (Check for district policy regarding prior approval for distributing flyers and publicity.) Communication is essential to the attendance and success of the event. Being part of the planning team validates the students' experiences and advocates for improved mental health.

8. At the completion of the event, the students, parents, and teachers should have the opportunity to evaluate successes. Possible prompts may include: Which parts of the collaboration were most successful? What was most problematic? What would you do differently if you could start over and do it again?

KEY TAKEAWAYS

♦ When school personnel suspect or have knowledge that a student has a disability, they must evaluate the student.

♦ Any evaluation must be multidisciplinary, nonbiased, and address all areas where there is suspicion that the student is having difficulty.

♦ The parents play an important role in the evaluation team.

♦ The evaluation team must determine whether the student has a disability, whether the student's disability has an adverse impact on their educational performance, and what type of services the student needs. The team must also determine the strengths of the student.

♦ In designing accommodations, the team must determine the preferences of the student and whether the student knows how to utilize the accommodations.

REFERENCES

Americans with Disabilities Amendments Act of 2008 (Public Law 110–325).

Artichoker v. Todd County School District, 69 IDELR 58 (D.S.D. 2016).

Hulett, K. (2009). *Legal aspects of special education.* Upper Saddle River, NJ: Merrill.

Individuals with Disabilities Education Act Statute (2004). 20 U.S.C. Section 1401.

Individuals with Disabilities Education Act Regulations (2004). 34 CFR 300.502(c)(1).

Johns, B. (2016). *Your classroom guide to special education law.* Baltimore, MD: Brookes.

Kauffman, J., & Badar, J. (2018). *The scandalous neglect of children's mental health: What schools can do.* New York, NY: Routledge.

Kline, J. (2017). *You be the judge: IDEA case studies for staff compliance training.* Palm Beach Gardens, FL: LRP.

Murdick, N., Gartin, B., & Crabtree, T. (2007). *Special education law.* Upper Saddle River, NJ: Pearson Education.

P.P v. Compton Unified School District, 235 F.Supp 3d 1126 (C.D. Cal., 2015).

Rehabilitation Act (1973). 29 U.S.C. Section 794.

Robinson, D. (2016). Might the ADA and Rehabilitation Act require accommodation of the effects of trauma in education under the ADA and Section 504. *Children's Rights Litigation, 18(2)*, 1–2.

San Diego Unified School District. 111 LRP 15918 (SEA CA 02/23/11).

Slater, A. (2017). *The special education 2017 desk book.* Palm Beach Gardens, FL: LRP.

Sulkowski, M., Joyce, D., & Storch, E. (2012). Treating childhood anxiety in schools: Service delivery in a response to intervention paradigm. *Journal of Child and Family Studies, 21*, 938–947.

PART IV
Resources for Educators

14

Resources for Further Study

Books for Adults

Gerber, B. L., & Guay, D. (Eds.). (2014). *Reaching and teaching students with special needs through art*. Alexandria, VA: National Art Education Association.

Gerber, B. L., & Kellerman, J. (2010). *Understanding students with autism through art*. Alexandria, VA: National Art Education Association.

Hunter, A., Heise, D., & Johns, B. (2018). Art for children experiencing psychological trauma: A guide for art educators and school-based professionals. New York, NY: Routledge.

Johns, B. (2016). *Your classroom guide to special education law*. Baltimore, MD: Brookes.

Kauffman, J., & Badar, J. (2018). *The scandalous neglect of children's mental health: What schools can do*. New York, NY: Routledge.

Books for Teenagers

Daniels, N. (2016). *Anxiety sucks! A teen survival guide*. CreateSpace North Charleston, SC: Independent Publishing Platform.

Green, J. (2017). *Turtles all the way down*. New York, NY: Penguin Young Readers Group.

Hide, M. O., & Forsyth, E. H. (2008). *Stress 101: An overview for teens.* Minneapolis, MN: Twenty-First Century Books (CT).

Robbins, A. (2006). *The overachievers: The secret lives of driven kids.* New York, NY: Hachette Books.

Saltzman, A. (2016). *A still quiet place.* Oakland, CA: New Harbinger.

Shannon, J., & Shannon, D. (Illustrator) (2015). *The anxiety survival guide for teens.* Oakland, CA: New Harbinger.

Children's Books

Cain, J. (2000). *The way I feel.* New York, NY: Parenting Press.

Cook, J. (2012). *Wilma Jean the worry machine.* Chattanooga, TN: National Center for Youth Issues.

Curtis, J. L., & Cornell, E. (Illustrator) (1998). *Today I feel silly and other moods that make my day.* New York, NY: Harper Collins.

Dismonty, M., & Shaw, K. (Illustrator) (2008). *Spaghetti in a hot dog bun.* Wixom, MI: Cardinal Rule Press.

Guanci, A. M., & Atta, C. (Illustrator) (2007). *David and the worry beast: Helping children cope with anxiety.* Far Hills, NJ: New Horizon Press.

Halloran, J. (2016). *Coping skills for kids workbook.* CreateSpace Independent Publishing Platform.

Romain, T., & Verdick, E. (2000). *Stress can get on your nerves.* Minneapolis, MN: Free Spirit Publishing.

Santat, D. (2007). *After the fall: How Humpty Dumpty got back up again.* New York, NY: Roaring Brook Press.

Snyder, B. & Shoults, A. (Illustrator) (2013). *Angel Violet's magic wings.* Chesterfield, MO: Mira Digital.

Waber, B. (2002). *Courage.* Boston, MA: Houghton Mifflin Harcourt.

Yamada, K., & Besom, M. (Illustrator) (2016). *What do you do with a problem?* Philadelphia, PA: Compendium.

Organizations

The American Academy of Child and Adolescent Psychiatry. Retrieved on December 19, 2018 from www.aacap.org. Started in 1900, the American Academy of Child and Adolescent Psychiatry (AACAP) promotes healthy development of children through advocacy education and research.

The Anxiety Disorder Resource Center of AACAP. Retrieved on December 19, 2018 from www.aacap.org. The Anxiety Disorder Resource Center of AACAP contains a plethora of resources specific to anxiety, including fact sheets for parents with children who experience anxiety.

Anxiety and Depression Association of America (ADAA). Retrieved on November 12, 2018 from http://adaa.org (home page). Founded in 1979, ADAA is an international nonprofit organization dedicated to the prevention, treatment, and cure of anxiety, depression, obsessive-compulsive disorder, post-traumatic stress disorder, and co-occurring disorders through education, practice, and research. ADAA focuses on improving quality of life for those with these disorders. ADAA provides education about the disorders and helps people find treatment, resources, and support.

Anxiety, Depression and Children's Mental Health, Centers for Disease Control and Prevention. Retrieved on December 19, 2018 from https://www.cdc.gov/childrensmentalhealth/depression. Contains information on anxiety including definitions, symptoms, treatments, and prevention.

Anxiety.org. Retrieved on December 19, 2018 from https://www.anxiety.org. This organization is committed to making mental health information accessible, inclusive, easy to find, and understand. The website contains relevant research on the full spectrum of anxiety and related disorders.

Council for Exceptional Children (CEC). Retrieved on December 19, 2018 from http://cec.sped.org. An international professional association of educators dedicated to advancing the success of children with exceptionalities. Its mission is accomplished through advocacy, standards, and professional development.

Council for Exceptional Children, Division of the Council for Children with Behavioral Disorders. Retrieved on January 14, 2019 from www.ccbd.net. The mission of this division is to advocate and promote the education and welfare of students with emotional/behavioral disorders. The division also provides workshops, has subdivisions in several states, and provides designated sessions at the CEC convention annually.

Council for Exceptional Children, Division of Visual and Performing Arts (DARTS). Retrieved on January 9, 2019 from http:community.cec.sped.org. Its mission is to advocate for arts education for individuals with exceptionalities; advance experiences with visual and performing arts for individuals with exceptionalities; foster collaboration among special educators, arts educators, arts therapists, and national arts education associations; promote professional community of educators in the fields of visual and performing arts education, arts therapy, and community arts organizations that work with individuals with exceptionalities; and encourage research about and disseminate information related to exemplary arts education for individuals with exceptionalities.

National Alliance on Mental Illness (NAMI). Retrieved on January 9, 2019 from https://www.nami.org. NAMI is the nation's largest grassroots mental health organization dedicated to building better lives for the millions of Americans affected by mental illness.

National Art Education Association, Special Needs Interest Group (NAEA/SNAE). Retrieved on January 9, 2019 from http://www.arteducators.org. A SNAE of the NAEA devoted to the promotion of art education for learners with special needs through professional development, educational collaboration, advancement of knowledge, and leadership.

Positive Behavioral Interventions & Supports (PBIS). Retrieved on November 21, 2018 from www.pbis.org (home page). PBIS is funded by the U.S. Department of Education's Office of Special Education Programs (OSEP) and the Office of Elementary and Secondary Education (OESE). Its Technical Assistance Center supports schools, districts, and states to build systems capacity for implementing a multi-tiered approach to social, emotional, and behavioral support. The main purpose of PBIS is to improve effectiveness, efficiency, and equity of schools and other agencies. PBIS improves social, emotional, and academic outcomes for all students with disabilities and students from underrepresented groups.

PESI. Retrieved on January 9, 2019 from www.pesi.com. PESI is a nonprofit organization, with a long history in the continuing education seminar business dating back to 1979. PESI is an accredited provider of continuing education by national accrediting agencies, including AOTA, ASHA, and numerous state physical therapy boards. Includes extensive list of self-regulation strategies.

PSYCOM. Retrieved on November 12, 2018 from http://www.
psycom.net (about us). Founded by Ivan K. Goldberg, MD, in
1997, initially as a discussion group for mental health professionals, Psycom.net has grown into a resource for a wide variety of mental health conditions, including bipolar disorder,
schizophrenia, depression, and generalized anxiety disorder.
Psycom.net seeks to educate and empower patients and caregivers to better understand their mental health condition and
to take an active role in their own care.

Understood. Retrieved on January 9, 2019 from https://www.
understood.org. A partnership of 15 nonprofit organizations
that joined forces to support parents with children with learning and attention issues. Includes a variety of free resources
and supports, including practical tips and access to experts
in the field.

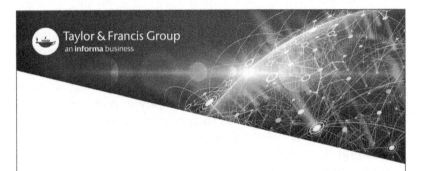

Made in the USA
Coppell, TX
18 September 2021